VISUALS of SC

C000140058

The Unconventional Tour Guide

30 years of travels around Scotland researching and painting places of special interest whilst discovering the true history, the unusual and the totally bizarre. Includes many personally experienced travel tips

illustrated & written by

Alastair M Carmichael

Aug 2005   Duntulm Castle

First published 30 May 2021 by Carmichael (Scotia) Ltd, Dalkeith, Scotland
Copyright © Alastair M Carmichael, Carloway, Isle of Lewis
art@carmichaelscotland.co.uk

PROLOGUE

Scotland is of course one of the most magnificent countries in the world with enviable landscapes, history and culture, albeit not so much enviable weather, and I have long considered myself most fortunate to have always lived here in my homeland despite decades of necessary foreign travel all over the globe which in truth confirmed my desire never to actually live anywhere else. There is an abundance to see, learn and experience in this ancient and hugely varying land with it's thousands of years of fascinating and frequently turbulent history which indeed one can get quite hooked on.

This book contains a selection of my drawings and paintings done between 1991 and 2021 (with a few some 20 years earlier) after visiting, exploring and researching a variety of some of Scotland's most unique, interesting and historic locations over a somewhat spread out 30 year period, albeit I must confess that most of these visuals were actually done not on location but at home near Edinburgh or up on the Isle of Lewis with plentiful supporting supplies of merlot and Tennents lager, whilst working from the numerous photos I had taken of each location to truly understand the detail and structure involved and whether using drawing pen & ink, watercolour or gouache was to be the most appropriate medium for the subject. Likewise there was much deliberation over the most suitable supporting alcoholic beverages.

The only place I have not personally visited in the book is the Flannan Isles, the place of the unsolved mystery of the three missing lighthouse keepers on those remote rocks in the wild Atlantic, and also there are a few imaginary visuals included in Mindscapes.

Please note that the images of the Saltire relate to Scotland's rich history and are in no way connected with the irresponsible hi-jacking by a certain political movement. After all a country's flag represents the nation as a whole and all of it's people and not various political parties of the moment.

I can only hope that these humble efforts entice both visitors and fellow Scots alike to explore the grandeur of this Scotland but if it is stately homes and posh gardens you want, sorry but this ain't the book for you, and also it is only fair to advise that herein contains some controversial albeit true facts and in doing so addresses several misconceptions in Scottish history.

For any further information please contact me on art@carmichaelscotland.co.uk

Yours aye

Alastair M Carmichael ~ 30 May 2021

AUTHOR'S NOTE: This book is **not** recommended for those easily offended, Bonnie Prince Charlie admirers, and sensitive Campbells.

CONTENTS

	Page	Map Ref
Prologue	ii	
Map	vi	
DISTILLERIES	**1**	
Ben Nevis	2	1
Cragganmore	4	2
Dalwhinnie	6	3
Glenmorangie	8	4
Lagavulin	10	5
Talisker	12	6
Classic Malts	14	
CASTLES	**15**	
Borthwick	16	7
Cardoness	18	8
Corgarff	20	9
Dalhousie	22	10
Dirleton	24	11
Duart	26	12
Dunnottar	28	13
Dunstaffnage	30	14
Dunvegan Castle	32	15
Edinburgh	34	16
Eilean Donan	36	17
Fenton	38	18
Gloom (Castle Campbell)	40	19
Hailes & Traprain Law	42	20
Hermitage	44	21
Inveraray - Inveraray Moon	46	22
Inveraray - Seat of Mac Cailein Mór	47	22
Lochindorb	48	23
Stalker - The Chiefs of Appin	50	24
Tantallon	52	25
Stalker	54	24

	Page	Map Ref

HEBRIDEAN HISTORY — 55

Callanish Stones - The Night Watch	56	*26*
Carloway Broch	58	*27*
Gearrannan Blackhouse Village - Croft House	60	*28*
Gearrannan Blackhouse Village - The High Street	61	*28*
Impressions of Lewis	62	
Impressions of Harris	63	
Loch Seaforth	64	*29*
Gearrannan Blackhouse Village - Midnight	66	*28*

MINDSCAPES — 67

Boat to No-Where	68
Coastal Croft	69
Harris Beach	70
Land of Grey & Pink - Caravan	70
Isolation	71
Wee Tigs Beach	72

SCOTTISH HISTORY — 73

Battle of Bannockburn - The Anxious Garrison	74	*30*
Battle of Bannockburn - The War Sword	76	*30*
Battle of Killiecrankie - The Soldier's Leap	78	*34*
Killiecrankie - Pass of Killiecrankie	79	*34*
Glencoe Massacre - The Three Sisters & Memorial	80	*32*
Glencoe Massacre - The Ruins of Glencoe	81	*32*
Glenfinnan Monument - Arrival at Glenfinnan....the '45	82	*33*
Glenfinnan Monument - Monument to a Fool	83	*33*
Battle of Culloden - Blood Skies Over Culloden	84	*31*
Hadrian's Wall - Keeping the Caledonians Out	86	*35*
Kilmartin - Guardians of Ballymeanoch	88	*36*
Kilmartin - Sentinals at Kilmartin	89	*36*
Peel of Lumphanan - Death of MacBeth	90	*37*
Kilmartin - Gateway to Kilmartin Glen	92	*36*

	Page	Map Ref

OUTLANDER LOCATIONS — 93

Callanish Stones - The Mists of Time .... 94 — 26
Callanish Stones - Piper at the Gates of Dawn .... 95 — 26
Battle of Culloden - The Last Dusk Afore Battle .... 96 — 31
Doune Castle - Castle Leoch .... 98 — 38
Midhope Castle - Lallybroch .... 100 — 39
Callanish Stones - Rock Solid .... 102 — 26

ISLE OF SKYE — 103

Old Man of Storr - Blue Horizons .... 104 — 40
Old Man of Storr - Cold Man of Storr .... 105 — 40
Old Man of Storr - Guardian of Trotternish .... 106 — 40
Old Man of Storr - Lucifer meets Storr .... 106 — 40
Elgol .... 107 — 41
Skye Coastal Croft 108

MYSTERY — 109

Ballachulish Gibbet - The Appin Murder .... 110 — 42
Bennane Cave - Cave of the Cannibals .... 112 — 43
Flannan Isles - The Missing Lighthouse Keepers .... 114 — 44
Loch Ness - Nessie & the Lorry Driver .... 116 — 45
Drumlanrig Castle - The Nicked da Vinci .... 118 — 46

GHOSTS — 119

Melrose Abbey - The Melrose Vampire .... 120 — 47
Coeffin Castle, Lismore - Return to Norway .... 122 — 48
Duntulm Castle - Mad MacDonald's final view .... 124 — 49
Greyfriars Graveyard - The Evil Judge Mackenzie .... 126 — 50

Epilogue 128

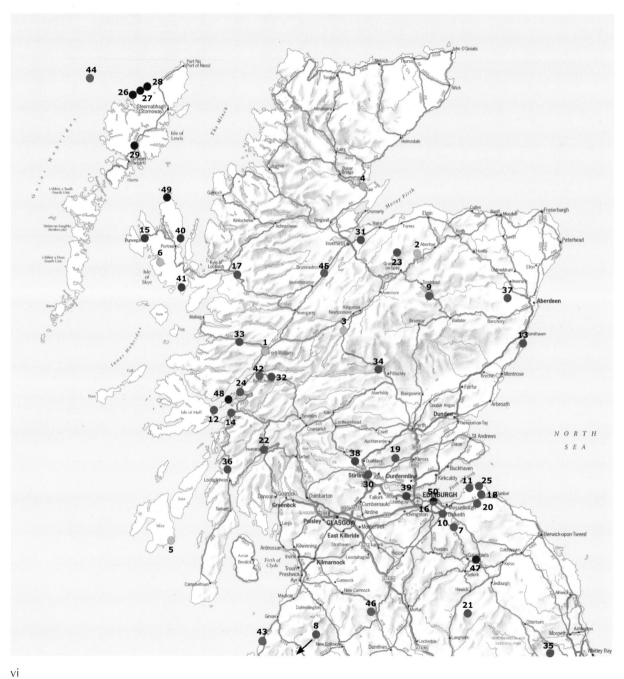

DISTILLERIES

Creating
The Water of Life

When building a distillery at the foot of Britain's highest mountain the founder would have the dilemma of coming up with the best name for that tipple yet to be produced. Mountainside Moonshine maybe or Scotch Mist but no, common sense prevailed and Ben Nevis started production in 1825 by one Long John MacDonald, a descendant of the unruly MacDonald Lords of the Isles, and he firstly produced Long John's Dew of Ben Nevis. A rival distillery simply named Nevis Distillery started in 1878 but soon it became apparent that rather than competing these two should merge to satisfy increasing demand which they did in the early 20th century. In Ben Nevis' history the distillery has been closed twice but under the current ownership the brand has much developed and continues to do so.

The real Ben Nevis which towers above the distillery with it's peak frequently shrouded in mist or covered in snow is 1,345 metres (4,410 ft) but unlike many other mountains the summit is relatively easy to reach trekking up a well trodden 4 mile path called the Mountain Track with no ropes, tackles and Sherpas required and with the additional benefit of a cafe at the top providing refreshments for all those worn out 'Edmund Hillarys'. In fact there are major concerns as to damage being done to the Ben with the thousands who climb it every year with the trek up taking approximately 4 hours. However, that is not to make light of it all. Poor weather can seriously affect visibility and avalanches and rock falls are not uncommon and due to such over the years quite a few folk have met their fate on Nevis. Every year not a few are rescued by the volunteering and dedicated Lochaber Mountain Rescue Team. For the more serious and experienced climber the North Face is the challenge and this climb is definitely not for the amateur. On the global scale, however, Ben Nevis is some would say quite titchy as Everest stands at 8,850 metres (29,030 ft), being almost seven times higher.

The distillery is on the outskirts of Fort William at the junction which leads out west to Glenfinnan. The principal single malt is the Ben Nevis 10 year old although 16 and 21 year olds are also available. The whiskies tend to be rather strong and intense with a spicy aroma leaving a pleasant malty finish, all of which can be sampled in the visitor centre.

Jan 2021

CRAGGANMORE DISTILLERY

Lovers of Speyside single malts could spend months in the region (followed by months in the divorce courts) with some 50 distilleries within easy mileage (this being approx one third of the 150 plus distilleries in Scotland), although visiting drivers should watch some of those tight bends on the roads in Speyside with the numerous whisky tanker lorries hurtling along at high speed transporting the 'Water of Life' down to the bottling plants in central Scotland. In fact Glenfiddich is the only Speyside distillery with a bottling line on site or this certainly was the case a few years ago.

Cragganmore is one of the six Diageo (formerly United Distillers) Classic Malts, slightly surprising as when you arrive at the distillery you tend to feel more that you have come across a rambling farm steading than a producer of this well known single malt scotch although in fact most production from this distillery is used for blended whiskies including White Horse regarding which a totally true story comes to mind. A white horse went into a pub in Glasgow and ordered a pint of Tennents lager. The curious landlord then said "That's strange, you drinking beer after they named a famous whisky after you", to which the horse responded "What? Eric?"

The distillery was founded by one John Smith (yup, honest) in 1869 and to reveal the popularity of this tipple from such a small distillery, in 1887 a dedicated 'whisky cargo only' train transported some 300 casks of Cragganmore east to Aberdeen.

To cater for increased production the distillery was rebuilt in 1902 and further extended in 1964 although it all still has that rather agricultural appearance.

The Cragganmore is quite a dry light tasting whisky with a clean and delicate palate with woody malty notes. Highly recommended is the Classic Malts 12 year old.

Oct 2020

5

DALWHINNIE DISTILLERY

A well known landmark for folk driving up and down the A9 Perth to Inverness road, and passing those isolated whitewashed buildings of Dalwhinnie distillery situated amongst the remote hills and mountains of the Cairngorms and Monadhlaiths. The name Dalwhinnie is derived from the Gaelic for a meeting place, lonely and isolated as it might clearly be but in days gone by, there were such meeting places around the Highlands with inns and basic accommodation where the drovers met and rested when taking their sheep and cattle livestock south to the markets in central Scotland and indeed it was not only drovers who used this route but gangs of whisky smugglers cunningly avoiding the authorities so eager to catch and prosecute them.

There is a small village of the same name just on the outskirts and it is hard to say whether the distillery is on the outskirts of the village or vice versa. The main Edinburgh to Inverness railway line runs directly behind the distillery and what a lonely little station is located there although in years past this was an essential transport link for bringing in materials and despatching casks both south and north. The distillery was built in 1897, badly damaged by fire in 1934 and re-opened four years later.

Dalwhinnie is a most pleasant and smooth single malt with a slight peaty taste, and also is the Classic Malt from the Highland Region.

Oct 2020

7

GLENMORANGIE DISTILLERY

For many years an aged photograph of The Sixteen Men of Tain in their work togs was used as an eye catching magazine advert for Glenmorangie single malt highlighting that whilst there are hundreds of folk sitting at computer screens in open plan offices throughout the Scottish central belt busy tapping away in their accounts, purchasing, logistics, distribution, administration, marketing, personnel and god-knows-what-else departments, those far away distilleries each have only a handful of people who actually produce the Water of Life.

Also advertised as coming from the Glen of Tranquility (not to be confused with the Sea of Tranquility on the Moon where moonshine was originally distilled) Glenmorangie has for most years since 1983 been Scotland's best selling single malt which is quite understandable with it's light, slightly sweet, slightly spicy taste and to bear this out some 10 million bottles are sold each year bottled at their plant in West Lothian. Ardbeg from Islay is also bottled on the same site as both brands share the same owner. It is also worth mentioning that Glenmorangie uses the tallest stills in Scotland at 8 metres (26 ft) high which helps create the light taste (according to the head distiller).

Located at Tain in Ross-shire north of Inverness, illicit booze was first produced on the Morangie Farm way back in 1703 and in 1730s a brewery was built at the farm's water source although this was much later in 1843 converted to a distillery by William Matheson who also renamed it Glenmorangie (albeit it is nowhere near any glen but on the shores of the Dornoch Firth). Like many distilleries it faced tough times particularly during Prohibition in the old colony and more recently with ridiculously high import tariffs courtesy of Donald Trump clearly so proud of his Scottish background, (see Gearrannan Blackhouses) again regarding exporting scotch into the old colony. Two months into the new Presidency in March 2021, Joe Biden intelligently removed the crucifying tariff which had reduced scotch exports to the USA by 35%.

The distillery was actually mothballed in both the 1930s and 1940s but since those dark days, however, the distillery has seen much expansion even taking the number of employees in Tain to a staggering two dozen (which is probably less than the canteen staff at head office).

Whilst there are excellent 12, 14, 18 and 25 year olds, the 10 year old is the heart of the range and any good drinks cabinet looks somewhat bare without this tipple taking up a prime position.

March 2021

9

LAGAVULIN DISTILLERY

There are few more appealing short trips away from home than a long weekend on Islay, a none too large island off the West Coast and home to 9 distilleries and a few thousand sheep and cattle. The 16 year old Lagavulin (another of the Classic Malts) is a favourite tipple for many with it's peat-rich smoky flavour, that being typical of the other Islay malts albeit to varying degrees, and yet all those others have their own distinctive unique flavours. Those others being Ardbeg, Bowmore, Bruichladdich, Bunnahabhain, Caol Ila, Kilchoman (the most recent), Laphroaig, and Port Ellen. Generally the Islay malts are dry and peaty and those 3 distilleries on the southern shoreline Laphroaig, Lagavulin and Ardbeg produce phenolic whiskies with aromas distinctive of tar, smoke, iodine and carbolic. Clearly not for the faint hearted and definitely an acquired taste.

Jura is the sole distillery on the adjacent island of Jura and can only be reached by a small ferry from Islay on a crossing of a few minutes. Having visited the distillery take a trip to see the Paps of Jura (no skool boy sniggering here please).

Like so many other distilleries, Lagavulin was founded by a farmer-come-distiller, this one by John Johnson in 1816 who found whisky more enjoyable than potatoes. The name is abbreviated Gaelic for 'the hollow where the mill is' and it is claimed that in the mid 1700s there were over 10 illicit whisky stills around the bay where Lagavulin is situated with it's close neighbours Laphroaig and Ardbeg on either side each only a mile away. The distillery's water rushes down from a stream gathering peat on it's journey to provide that essential taste characteristic. It is one of only a few distilleries where the jetty still juts out into the sea for past shipping in of materials and shipping out of filled casks although these days everything is trucked on and off the island by CalMac's ferry and principally by one haulier well established for this lucrative transport business.

Islay can be reached either by the Caledonian MacBrayne ferry MV Finlaggan with an approx two hour crossing from Kennacraig or Loganair's flight from Glasgow which at somewhat higher prices is more suited to distilling companies personnel than the average traveller, whilst the CalMac ferry has the added advantage of you filling the boot (trunk for the Yanks) with a substantial supply of the Water of Life and all manner of other goodies from the distillery shops (allegedly as presents but mainly for you). In order to tour all of the distilleries properly (rather than quick pop ins) 3 days are needed on Islay as the lengthy tours and tasting sessions can overlap between distilleries on certain days and some are a fair distance from each other. Unless some poor sod is tasked with driving those who are having the fun, it is highly recommended to agree a daily rate with one of the island's taxi companies even though much of the time the driver will be parked up eating his wife's egg mayo sarnies whilst you and your companions spend ages sniffing, snorting and tasting a selection of various malts whilst making various mind-bending and bizarre comments regarding respective palates before staggering back out to the taxi and hopefully getting in the right one.

Oct 2020

TALISKER DISTILLERY

Until quite recently, Talisker was the only distillery on the Isle of Skye but two newcomers have since taken away that monopoly these being Torabhaig and Isle of Raasay. Started by two MacAskill brothers in 1830 Talisker soon passed into other hands and various other owners with one more than eager or rather crooked sales agent sent to jail for selling non existent casks of whisky, albeit such tales are not uncommon in the development and goings on in the whisky distilling business, mostly illicit in the 1700s and 1800s (see Corgarff Castle).

This single malt has a peppery character and has been described by expert whisky tasters as 'The lava of the Cuillins' and also 'it explodes on the palate'.

Robert Louis Stevenson looked upon Talisker as his favourite scotch, along with Glenlivet..........and er, also all of the Islay whiskies. After all you would need a bit of good stuff to stir the imagination whilst writing Treasure Island, Dr Jekyll and Mr Hyde, and Kidnapped.

Diageo has owned Talisker for many years now and the distillery is a 'must visit' for many who tour Skye (not quite so much the Isle of Skye now since the bridge replacing the ferries opened in 1995) particularly as the distillery's coastal views at Carbost are quite magnificent.

Some tasters describe Talisker's palate as lively with rich plummy fruits, chocolate and cinder toffee combined with smoke, with a finish of sweet malt biscuit with more smoke. Who the hell comes up with this stuff? Are we actually talking about scotch here? Or biscuits? Having said that Talisker is a bloody good single malt and particularly recommended is Talisker Storm which does hold a powerful, spicy taste, whilst the 10 year old is one of the Classic Malts.

Oct 2020

LAGAVULIN

DALWHINNIE

CRAGGANMORE

TALISKER

Bha càileachd an uisge-beatha na b'fheàrr na càileachd an luchd-obrach

CASTLES

Scotland's Defences

BORTHWICK CASTLE

Built in 1430 by Sir William Borthwick, 1st Lord of Borthwick this castle located some 12 miles south of Edinburgh in Midlothian is an impressionable fortress over 35 metres high (115 ft) with walls 5 metres (16 ft) thick, honeycombed throughout with stairways and chambers. The castle is protected on three sides by the convergence of two rivers, with the 4th side originally being safeguarded by a moat.

A month after their marriage in 1567, Mary Queen of Scots and her third husband and likely the only one she ever loved, James Hepburn, 4th Earl of Bothwell sought sanctuary here, but both had to escape, with the advance of the Confederate Lord's army politically opposed to this impulsive marriage. The Queen escaped disguised as a male servant, and had to be lowered from the Great Hall window by a rope, and quite alone crossed the rough country through the dark night to find Bothwell, who in hardly a chivalrous fashion had already scarpered, having left his Queen behind in Borthwick. Their last days of freedom together had been spent secure in Borthwick, but such togetherness was not destined to be for long. The beginning of the end took place only a month after their marriage, at the Battle of Carberry Hill in East Lothian where Bothwell's army of 2,000 met the Confederate Lord's army of a similar size, the latter force winning the day. Bothwell deserted the battle and returned to his Dunbar Castle for tea and Jaffa Cakes, whilst Mary accepting the royalist defeat, surrendered herself to the Lords.

In 1650 Borthwick Castle was besieged by Oliver Cromwell who had invaded Scotland with his huge English Parliamentarian army consisting of thousands of highly trained and superbly armed professional soldiers. Thus, instead of the normal combination of personal troops led by various conflicting and feuding lords and nobles, this was the first truly national military machine and much to be feared. The Scottish Parliament had done something of a u-turn and was now fully supporting Charles II as King of both Scots and England, and such decision had prompted a heavy military response from Cromwell who marched northwards. En route on his destructive path, he stopped and wrote to the 8th Lord of Borthwick, a royalist supporter stating "I thought fitt to send this trumpett to you, to lett you know that, if you please to walk away with your company, you shall have liberties to carry off your arms and goods. You harboured such parties in your house as have basely, unhumanely murdered our men; if you necessitate me to bend my cannon against you, you must expect what I doubt you will not be pleased with. I expect your present answer, and rest your servant, O.Cromwell". When no response came forthwith, 'his servant', O.Cromwell proceeded to bombard Borthwick with his heavy artillery until it's Lord rather wisely surrendered his castle. The cannon fire destroyed the parapet on the east face, and damage in the upper wall is still very much in evidence today. Cromwell honourably kept his word as not only did he allow Lord Borthwick, his family, and garrison to depart without any hindrance, he actually gave them 2 weeks to clear all their possessions out of the castle, before occupying the place with his own troops.

Certain Lords of Borthwick of a particularly nasty disposition, forced prisoners, with their hands tied behind their backs, to jump the 4 metres (13 ft) gap between the 2 high towers. Success (on very seldom occasion) resulted in freedom (maybe) whereas failure (on almost every occasion) resulted in the unfortunate jumpers being impaled upon spikes suitably positioned 35 metres (115 ft) below, the gardeners having to rake up a bit more than the usual autumn leaves.

During the Second World War, the castle's impregnable vaults were used to shelter many of Scotland's art treasures and precious documents from the Luftwaffe (now Lufthansa Airlines), who had somewhat less success at damaging Borthwick than Cromwell had achieved some 300 years previously.

Borthwick is reputed to have two resident ghosts, one of a serving wench who was made a little bit pregnant by one of the Borthwick Lords, and after producing his little bastard son, she was a little bit murdered. Most certainly, one way out of paying alimony, or having to tell all those fibs to Lady Borthwick on one's whereabouts last October. The second ghost concerns an individual who was caught doing some creative accounting regarding the Borthwick family's affairs and accounts. He found himself in hot water, or rather hot flames when he was burned alive at the stake after his misdemeanors were discovered.

The castle recently refurbished at great cost is an excellent place to stay for a luxuriously historic few days with superb rooms and fine dining in the Great Hall whilst also being a highly recommended venue for events and gatherings (personally experienced).

In 2020, 21 years after drawing this, the 24th Lord & Lady Borthwick visited us to order some items with this image.

Feb 1999

CARDONESS CASTLE

Most castles in Scotland and indeed England were built not for national defence and war mongering activities between these two long standing rival nations, but much more for personal protection and security against hostile neighbours hell bent on raiding, stealing, rape, and that old feuding favourite, slaughter of the enemy, frequently being, yes, your neighbour. Certainly somewhat different from today's typical problems with a neighbour who does not take his rubbish out on Tuedays, or parks his camper van on the edge of your lawn, or even worse lets his dog crap on your lawn. Galloway covering much of south west Scotland was no exception to these feuds, and thus there are, in various states of condition, dozens of castles and tower houses throughout the region. Cardoness, still in excellent condition, is one of these, built in the late 1400s by the McCullochs, a powerful Galloway family who had quite a track record for causing mayhem and trouble, those being their better qualities, particularly with their Gordon neighbours with whom they were always in dispute over land ownership. The McCullochs acquired Cardoness through marriage after the previous laird drowned in a frozen loch in 1460 together with 8 of his 9 daughters and his new born son and heir. The sole surviving daughter married a McCulloch, and the 6 storey Cardoness Castle was built by Gilbert McCulloch, 1st Laird thereof. His son James McCulloch, 2nd Laird, was an unscrupulous fellow resorting to litigation over land ownership 5 times before his death in 1500, even when on occasion it was certainly not his land anyway. To acquire lands from the MacLellans, James had his only daughter marry the wealthy but retarded Alexander MacLellan, ending up in dispute with the lawful land owner who was in fact the Douglas Earl of Angus. For various nasty deeds James McCulloch was outlawed in 1471 and again in 1480. James' son Ninian McCulloch, 3rd Laird, whilst a sheriff depute, was also a rather bad fellow and extorted illegal rents from locals, and ultimately was executed in 1509 for a number of crimes including stealing 1,500 cattle belonging to none other than his own father's widow. After Ninian's execution, Patrick MacLellan, brother of the wronged and inept Alexander, attacked Cardoness and evicted the McCullochs reclaiming the MacLellans rights, albeit the McCullochs took a dim view of this and soon Cardoness was back in McCulloch hands. Ninian's son, Cutlar McCulloch, 4th Laird spent much of his time constantly and brutally raiding the Isle of Man with the resultant prayer on the island, "God keep the good corn, sheep, and bullock from Satan, sin, and Cutlar McCullock".

Cardoness was built at the time when firearms and artillery were taking over from archery, and it was one of the first castles in Scotland which incorporated inverted-keyhole gun holes in the walls although most of the other features were typical of Scottish tower houses. One English spy who sketched Cardoness in 1565 for Elizabeth I's government intent on evaluating Scottish defences whilst considering yet another invasion of Scotland, reported that it would was highly defendable and would take 200 men to capture the place with a direct attack. The McCullochs were supporters of Mary Queen of Scots, albeit this was somewhat secondary to being supporters of themselves. Numerous clans did not have any true allegiances but conveniently used various times of war for pay back against rivals.

In 1628 the McCullochs heavily in debt following years of financial recklessness, high living and more than a few errors by William McCulloch, were forced to sell Cardoness to their neighbour John Gordon whom they hated with a vengeance as can soon be seen. Bearing grudges and refusing to accept their downward spiraling change of fortunes, years later in 1668, the McCullochs violently took possession of Cardoness, when Alexander McCulloch dragged John Gordon's fatefully ill widow from her sick bed and threw her to die on top of a mound of cattle muck. In 1690 his son Sir Godfrey McCulloch shot and killed William Gordon, the son of John Gordon. Sir Godfrey fled to France but 7 years later he was spotted strangely, as he was hardly religious, in St. Giles Cathedral in Edinburgh, and was promptly arrested and executed in Edinburgh on The Maiden, Scotland's earlier but less fanciful equivalent of the French guillotine. The penalty for his father interring the old lady in the shite was somewhat more lenient. He was only fined as presumably infringing some by-law.

Thus ended the 200 year dominance of the notoriously nasty McCullochs, and indeed the history of Cardoness Castle, although unlike Clan McCulloch, the castle is still in fine form.

Sept 2013

CORGARFF CASTLE

These rare days when the sun is out and shining brightly, Corgarff looks to be a most pleasant white painted tower house with a neatly built star shaped wall, whilst secretly harbouring excellent potential as a garden centre and cafeteria selling donuts and the like, but it's long turbulent history is much removed from anything pleasant. Way back in 1571 when Corgarff was held by a Forbes laird who continued a long standing feud against a branch of the powerful north eastern Gordons, one such Adam Gordon of Auchindoun, who had found out that Forbes and all of his men were away from home on some venture, ravaged the area and attacked Corgarff Castle. Margaret Campbell, wife of the laird refused to surrender, secured the castle, and from an upper window she shot one of the Gordons in the knee with a pistol. Furious at this act of unwarranted aggression (although let us remember that it was he who started this wee bit of bother), Adam Gordon then instructed his men to pile up and set alight wood against the main door, and also to light fires in the latrine (bog) chutes, resulting in the brave Margaret and 27 of her kinsfolk including children and servants being horribly burned to death. Gordon evaded prosecution for this hideous deed by claiming that he did such in the name of Mary Queen of Scots, whilst the Forbes clan apparently supported the government lords representing the rival claimant to the throne, being none other than Mary's own infant son James VI. These days one such as Adam Gordon would likely claim that he was urged / incited to do so by Donald Trump. Thus not much of an excuse for such a horrific offence, just like the raid on the Washington Capitol on 6 January 2021 when latterly over 300 non-Gordon raiders were arrested (little bit of politics there).

In 1607 a gang of Highland outlaws captured the castle and held it as their base for an unbelievable 20 years terrorising the local vicinity with stealing, rape and slaughter on their main agenda until John Erskine 3rd Earl of Mar, by brute force evicted this wild bunch in 1626. Another 20 years on, in 1645, the Marquis of Montrose mustered his royalist troops there, and years later in 1689 the royalists torched the place to prevent it being garrisoned by enemy government Hanoverian forces. The Jacobites mustered there again during the rebellion in 1715, and later that year in a turn of events the Hanoverian redcoats torched the place to prevent the Jacobites using it further as a meeting place for mustering armed forces. The Jacobites, however, did use it again much later during the final rebellion in 1746 as an ammunition store, but 400 government redcoats were despatched from Aberdeen, descended on Corgarff, wiped out the small Jacobite garrison and captured a huge supply of muskets and gun powder badly needed by the Jacobite army on their return from their long foray into England.

After the Battle of Culloden, Corgarff was occupied by 50 redcoats and the unique star shaped wall was built enabling it's garrison total protection and visibility of the surrounding landscape, with dozens of musket firing slits incorporated into the unique surrounding wall. Corgarff's function at that time was to enforce the Hanoverian government's harsh new laws intent on totally destroying all Highland clan culture, and brutally enforcing the ban on Highlanders carrying any weapons, and also bans on tartans, bagpipes, and shortbread tins. There was no need for the well designed defensive wall. Bonnie Prince Charlie had already totally fucked up the Jacobite cause so no more attacks would ever occur (see Battle of Culloden).

Corgarff's final use was in 1830s again as a government base but this time in attempts to control (with not particularly great success) the burgeoning activities in illegal whisky distillation which was fast becoming something of a lucrative hobby in the Highlands and simultaneously a major headache for the excise men.

CORGARFF
CASTLE.

AMC
26-6-92

June 1992

DALHOUSIE CASTLE

Few who arrive to stay at Dalhousie Castle not many miles south of Edinburgh realise the long and varied history this fortress has had outstripping many other castles, this being the seat of the Ramsays of Dalwolsey from when first built by an English knight Simon of Ramsey sometime after his arrival in Scotland in 1140 right up to 1900. Eventually selling the castle in 1977, the Ramsays had held the place for over 800 years the name dal-a'-h'oisinn being Gaelic for 'the dale at the corner'.

The first significant mention is when King Edward I of England aka Longshanks aka The Hammer of the Scots stayed there when on one his several major invasions into Scotland, this time in 1298 to suppress the rebel Scots led by Mel Gibson aka William Wallace.

One of the most renowned lords was Sir Alexander Ramsay, a prominent knight in defending Scotland from Edward III's invasion in 1335 and thereafter during the English occupation using guerilla warfare tactics to ambush enemy troops (inc rival Scots supporting the usurper Edward Balliol), harass and capture supply trains (pre ScotRail), and eventually to regain his Dalwolsey Castle which those pesky English had taken over. Tragically he was not killed honourably in battle but starved to death in a dungeon in the grim Hermitage Castle (see Hermitage Castle) by his former best friend Sir William Douglas, the Flower of Chivalry over the latter's anger that Ramsay had been appointed Sheriff of Teviotdale by the young King David II to replace Douglas and as reward for recapturing the royal borders castle of Roxburgh from the English in 1342. To compound his jealous outrage Douglas had failed several times to recapture Roxburgh.

Nigel Tranter the famous Scottish historical novelist and castles expert noted in his brilliant novel Flowers of Chivalry about Alexander Ramsay and Will Douglas, that the drum tower which housed the deep water well also had a most unusual feature that instead of the usual turnpike stair, the original stairway wound up to the top floor within the thickness of the wall.

In 1400 the castle withstood a 6 month siege by Henry IV of England clearly showing this castle's early strong fortifications although this Alexander was killed 2 years later at the ill fated Battle of Homildon Hill where the Scots army was annihilated by English archers having crazily taken up a defence position on a hill side. Another Alexander was killed at the Battle of Flodden in 1513. The Ramsays of Dalwolsey were truly loyal supporters to the Scots throne further borne out with the Ramsays fighting for Mary Queen of Scots at the Battle of Langside in 1568.

In 1633 William Ramsay was created the 1st Earl of Dalhousie and had the castle significantly extended again using locally quarried red sandstone.

Oliver Cromwell visited in 1648 but unlike most of his castle visits when invading Scotland he used it as his military base rather than bombarding the place to hell with cannon fire, such being a favourite hobby of Cromwell (see Borthwick & Dirleton Castles). When one enters the castle, the slots in the wall for the drawbridge chains are quite visible above the front door entrance clearly showing that the best defence is a narrow one horse only entrance and hardly like the huge wide drawbridges stormed by hundreds of minimum pay extras in many a film.

Before becoming a luxurious hotel in 1972 Dalhousie was in fact a boarding skool for a few decades from 1925, albeit one with a crap rugby team. The hotel handles many weddings a year. Some of those unions work out and some don't but in the latter case you won't get a booze refund from the hotel for your error of judgement. These days the grounds much to the benefit and delight of hotel guests houses a collection of birds of prey including falcons, hawks, owls and eagles and also for the delight of some and fear of others Dalhousie is home to a few ghosts including the Grey Lady, being a mistress of one of the Ramsay lords resulting in his somewhat spiteful wife starving her to death in one of the turrets. Another spook relates to the boarding skool period when a boy fell to his death when jumping from the battlements. The extent some lads go to in avoiding that horrible French exam. There is even a spectre of a dog who in 1980s fell to it's death so it is best to check in advance with reception on the hotel's pet policy.

Feb 2021

DIRLETON CASTLE

Since 1220 this medieval castle has nobly crowned the rocky outcrop in the picturesque village of Dirleton some 25 miles south east of Edinburgh. Originally built by John de Vaux to replace his earlier Castle Tarbet, which was built on the nearby island of Fidra in the Firth of Forth, the castle went through 3 major architectural developments, the first being with the de Vaux family in the 13th century, the second when the castle passed to the Halyburtons circa 1350, and lastly when it passed through marriage to the notorious Ruthvens in 1515.

In 1298, King Edward I of England invaded Scotland (again) to crush the nationalist uprising spearheaded by the common people's hero William Wallace (alias Mel Gibson). Dirleton Castle strategically threatened the right flank of the English army, and Edward ordered his brutal deputy, Anthony Beck, Bishop of Durham, to attack and take possession of the castle. Beck's initial siege proved fruitless and he lost many men as missiles, boiling liquid, lentil soup, and the like were poured down onto the English attackers. John de Vaux's plans to build the castle on the rocky knoll with the towers splayed out at the base had proved worthwhile, and had prevented the English forces from undermining the stonework to gain access. Eventually however, the English brought up huge siege engines and commenced heavy bombardment which the garrison could not withstand. Surrender ensued and Beck permitted the defenders to go free, an unusual act of leniency for that apparently religious, but notoriously cruel and harsh general.

In 1566 during the Ruthven ownership of Dirleton Castle, Patrick, 3rd Lord Ruthven, was the principal conspirator in the murder of David Rizzio, Mary Queen of Scots' secretary who many historians believe was her lover, and some with good reason suggest the real father of King James VI. Ruthven's son, a fellow conspirator in the plot, became William, Earl of Gowrie in 1581 and, the following year, in an attempt to break the Earl of Arran's control of the government, he captured and held the young King James VI prisoner and for some 10 months Gowrie and his conspirators controlled Scotland. The King, however, eventually escaped and the Earl of Gowrie was ultimately beheaded in 1585. 15 years later in 1600, John, 3rd and last Earl of Gowrie, son of the aforementioned Earl William, together with Sandy Ruthven, one of John's younger brothers were murdered having been set up by Sir Thomas Erskine for their involvement in the "Gowrie Conspiracy", an apparent but unlikely plot to assassinate James VI. At Gowrie House in Perth the King and his favourite page (at that moment in time as the King was a little bit gay) had led the two Ruthvens to an upper room to discuss a Treasury loan of £85,000 the former William, Earl of Gowrie had made the King, and the current Earl John wanted the debt repaid with interest. Pitiful yells of treason were heard from the agitated King and when the other lords burst into the room, the King was splattered in blood, albeit not his own, Ramsay the page held a bloodied dagger and both Ruthven brothers lay dead on the floor. Surprisingly thereafter the payday loan was never repaid even with the APR interest calculation of only 18,500%, being roughly equivalent to the U.S. defence budget. James VI was an extremely odd King, totally paranoid, insecure and who achieved very little in his 58 years on the thrones of both Scotland and ultimately England, than other than simply surviving. He was referred to as The Wisest Fool in Christendom, a justifiable title as despite his numerous failings, no-one could get rid of him. He died in 1625, peaceably rather than at the end of a blade unlike several far better Stewart monarchs. He was succeeded by his son Charles I who as history would show lacked the luck of his father. After the Gowrie Conspiracy, Dirleton's lands and castle were forfeited from Lady Ruthven and gifted to the aforesaid Sir Thomas Erskine by James VI, and thus became Lord Erskine of Dirleton. The remaining Ruthven offspring had wisely long since fled into England.

In 1649, the infamous DIRLETON WITCHES case occurred whereby ignorant and vindictive locals, most likely with personal grievances against their neighbours over noisy parties and dog fouling accused a group of innocent women and men as being in league with the Devil upon which they were duly arrested and held in the castle dungeon. After being forced under torture by the sadistic and typically lunatic witchfinder

John Kincaid (consider the similarity to Vincent Price in the great film Witchfinder General) to make various absurd confessions about their associations and tea parties with the Devil, they were sentenced to death by strangulation and thereafter burning at the stake on the village green.

In 1650 the castle came under attack for the final time when Oliver Cromwell's army was invading Scotland. The Dirleton garrison consisting of moss-troopers and royalist irregulars were constantly riding out and successfully attacking and destroying Cromwell's lines of supply. To end this, General Monk the English commander, led a division of 1,600 troops to Dirleton to lay it waste. The castle proved to be no match against Cromwell's artillery and one of the first shots severely damaged the drawbridge and entrance, also killing the lieutenant of the moss-troopers. The garrison thereafter surrendered handing over weapons and also 10 English prisoners. General Monk proved to be less forgiving than Beck had been those hundreds of years before, and shot 3 of the Scottish officers immediately after the surrender. The front wall of the castle still clearly reveals the damage resultant from Cromwell's artillery attack. The surrender of Borthwick Castle to Oliver Cromwell himself was clearly much more honourable than that to his own general at Dirleton. Since that outcome only time has played it's inevitable part in the further deterioration of this most impressive medieval fortress.

Nov 1999

DUART CASTLE

On the south eastern tip of the Isle of Mull built on a promontory known as Black Point stands Duart castle, strategically sited at the meeting point of 3 important seaways, the Firth of Lorne, Loch Linnhe, and the Sound of Mull, thus being in a prime location to control the shipping between the Hebrides and Ireland. There was a fort here in ancient times, but the existing castle has been (for most of the time) the ancestral seat of the Clan MacLean, since the 14th century. In 1411 Donald MacDonald, Lord of the Isles and his Highland clan and Islesmen allies including the MacLeans of Duart launched an offensive in the north of Scotland, Donald intent on foraying south and taking the throne of Scotland for himself. They were intervened by a much smaller army under Alexander Stewart, Earl of Mar, (son of the Wolf of Badenoch) on orders from the Duke of Albany, and the bloody Battle of Harlaw took place (see Dunvegan Castle). A notorious mortal combat took place in mid battle between the huge red headed and likewise red bearded, Hector, 6th Chief of MacLean, suitably named 'Red Hector of the Battles' and Sir Alexander Irvine of Drum who had most courageously challenged the dreaded MacLean chief, to distract the MacLean clansmen's onslaught, and buy some time for the Earl of Mar to change battle tactics. Despite Red Hector being regarded as one of the best swordsman in the land, with many rival combatant corpses to his name he was killed by Irvine, who shortly after, also died of his own injuries from that fatal combat.

In 1520s, Lachlan, 11th Chief of MacLean tried to murder his barren wife Margaret Campbell by tying her up and leaving her abandoned on a rock to be drowned by the rising tide. Believing her dead, he travelled to the Clan Campbell family seat in Inveraray to offer his condolences to her brother, the Campbell, Earl of Argyll, bringing with him a coffin full of turf claiming it to contain her body. On arrival at Inveraray Castle, much to his surprise, he found his wife at the head of the dining table with her brother. She had fortunately been rescued by a passing fishing boat. Campbell revenge was soon forthcoming and MacLean was stabbed to death by Sir John Campbell of Cawdor whilst sleeping in Edinburgh. In later years the Campbells would prove to be a much larger problem for the MacLeans.

For long the MacLeans had been vassals of the unruly MacDonalds, Lords of the Isles but with the Crown determined to destroy this constant threat, a plan was hatched to kidnap several Highland clan chiefs including Hector, Chief of MacLean. They were invited on board a royal ship for hospitality with the King's Lord Lieutenant upon which they were promptly arrested, the condition for Hector's release being destruction of his fleet of war galleys and loyalty to King James V. Thus the MacLeans, free from the past dominance of the MacDonald Lords of the Isles and those lord's hatred of the Crown, became staunch royalists.

An oath the MacLeans loyally kept, by fighting with the noble royalist general Marquis of Montrose against the government Covenanters, during which time the MacLeans took a short holiday and attacked the Campbell Earl of Argyll's, Castle Gloom, near Stirling, in 1645, burning and largely destroying their enemy's lowland fortress (see Castle Gloom). However, 2 years later Sir Lachlan MacLean lost in the fight against the competent General David Leslie's Covenanter's forces including Campbells which attacked Duart Castle in 1647. Thereafter the MacLeans lost many more clansmen at the Battle of Inverkeithing in 1651. In 1653, the surrounding waters of the Isle of Mull aided the MacLeans greatly when a violent storm sunk 2 of Oliver Cromwell's warships besieging Duart Castle. The MacLeans loyalty to the Crown continued during the Jacobite uprisings and the castle was again besieged in 1674 and 1688 by government forces.

Whilst most of the MacLeans under Sir John MacLean were far from home and involved in the first Jacobite battle and victory at the Battle of Killiecrankie in 1689 (see Battle of Killicrankie) under overall command of the able John Graham, 1st Viscount Dundee (who despite his victory was killed by a stray musket shot), things were not so good on the home front as now Campbell warships were attacking and bombarding Duart, with very few men left there to defend the castle. The MacLeans loyalty to King Charles and the royalist cause, and their hatred of the Campbells would cost them dear. The MacLeans lost Duart 2 years later in 1691 when the castle and all their lands on Mull were surrendered to the Campbell Duke (a sort of promotion from Earl) of Argyll. Thereafter redcoat troops garrisoned Duart until 1751, but they largely destroyed the castle on their departure to render it useless to any future opposition. From then on it remained empty and ruinous for 160 years.

It was not until 1910 that it was back in MacLean hands when Sir Fitzroy MacLean, 26th Chief, bought the castle and started on the costly extensive restoration.

DUART CASTLE ~ JMC 10.10.93

Oct 1993

DUNNOTTAR CASTLE

Without doubt Dunnottar Castle near Stonehaven and some 15 miles south of Aberdeen would have been the most impregnable fortress in Scotland, dominating the complete top area of a vast rocky monolith protruding high above the surrounding lowlands on one side and the icy cold waters of the North Sea on the other sides. Whilst the castle was built by Sir William Keith, Great Marischal of Scotland in 1290s, there had been a fort here as long ago as AD 681 when the Pictish King Bridei held out against a long siege by an enemy fleet from the Orkney Islands, and over 200 years later in AD 895 when King Donald II was killed here whilst defending the fort against the Vikings, who eventually captured and destroyed the fortress in AD 899 The next century in AD 934 Dunnottar, under command of King Constantine II withstood a 2 month siege waged by the southern warlord Athelstan of Wessex who was planning on adding Scotland to his rapidly expanding property portfolio. The original forts would of course have been built of earth and timber, and whilst the rock and the shear cliffs obviously provided much natural defence, it could be that some of the successful attacks were more due to treachery and betrayal than major assault.

The existing castle was barely complete before it fell into English hands under King Edward I, the Hammer of the Scots, in 1296. However, a year later in 1297, William Wallace (alias Mel Gibson) attacked Dunnottar and having trapped many of the English garrison inside the chapel, being those who had rather mistakenly sought sanctuary there, Wallace set the building alight, burning to death all those inside. Wallace and his men had secretly gained entry along a narrow rock ridge, which was wisely excavated away after the attack to ensure that such an approach could not be repeated. By 1336 Dunnottar was in English hands again when King Edward III of England sent 100 archers to protect the masons, carpenters and builders assigned to strengthening the castle's defences (for the English of course). Despite all these home improvements, Sir Andrew Moray with a Scots army ousted the English garrison in November of the same year and it returned to being held by a Scottish garrison much pleased with the enhanced defences kindly provided by the English King.

In 1645 the royalist general, Marquis of Montrose attacked the castle with the aim of capturing the Covenanter 7th Earl of Marischal, but failed, and thus in something of a foul mood he burnt down all the surrounding buildings and savaged the Earl's lands. The previous year Montrose with an army of 1,700 had soundly defeated a Covenanter army more than twice the size, at the Battle of Aberdeen so the population around the region justifiably feared the actions of the notable royalist.

So impregnable was this place that in 1651 the decision was made by the Scottish royalists to hide therein, the Honours of Scotland, the posh name for the Scottish Crown Regalia, to prevent Oliver Cromwell and the English Parliamentarian army capturing these most precious articles so soon after the coronation of Charles II as King of Scots (albeit not England yet) at Scone near Perth. After an incredible 8 month siege, even Dunnottar could not withstand the onslaught of the English artillery and the garrison reluctantly surrendered in May 1652. Some historians suggest the siege actually ended due more to a lack of sandwiches than the bombardment. Cromwell's Roundhead soldiers searched the castle throughout (notably without a warrant), but the Honours had long since gone and had in fact been smuggled out by one Mrs. Grainger, the local church minister's wife and had been buried under the floor of the nearby Kinneff parish church (that is the Honours, not Mrs Grainger). There they remained hidden for the next 9 years until it was considered safe to retrieve them. The Honours are now on display for all to see, safely secure in Edinburgh Castle. One of these items is the Papal sword being a beautifully crafted sword given to James IV by Pope Julius II in the early 1500s.

The little known Catholic James VII became King James VII of Scots & II of England in 1685, after the death of his brother Charles II, prompting an uprising from the Protestant Covenanters led by the Campbell, 9th Earl of Argyll who gathered armed forces at his Dunstaffnage Castle. The revolt was easily put down by royalist troops and 167 Covenanters were held at Dunstaffnage before being sent over the breadth of Scotland to Dunnottar Castle. The castle's last real use was thus in 1685 being a prison which held in atrocious conditions these 122 men and 45 women who had refused to accept the new Royal Prayer Book and they were incarcerated in the Whig's Vault. It was a most shameful episode in which several of the prisoners died of illness and malnutrition. So bad were the foul conditions that 25 prisoners escaped by climbing out of a window and down the shear precipice, several falling to their deaths on the rocks below. 15 were recaptured, locked in the gatehouse and tortured by having their fingers burnt to ashes, some of whom died of their injuries. The rest were shipped away as slaves destined for the West Indies. All of this horror because of their refusal to acknowledge a new prayer book. Oh yes, and a Christian one at that. The Campbell 9th Earl of Argyll was executed for treason in 1685 on the Maiden in Edinburgh, just like his father, 8th Earl (and Montrose's direst enemy) had been in 1661. The Maiden was a portable guillotine used in Scotland centuries before such an execution device was made fashionable during Le French Revolution.

The last Earl Marischal of Dunnottar was of a Jacobite persuasion and participated in the ill fated 1715 rebellion, resulting in his lands, estates and Dunnottar being forfeited and sold. Thereafter the castle was largely dismantled, although there is still much which can be seen today on it's prominent mass of rock.

July 1993

DUNSTAFFNAGE CASTLE

A fortress, the first being in 7th century, has strategically guarded Loch Etive for more than 1,500 years, originally being held by the ancient Scots of Dalriada, but always guarding and holding a principal route from the Argyll coast into central Scotland, much prone to the risk of landward invasion. The existing castle dates back to 1220 and was built by Duncan MacDougall, grandson of the Great Somerled, King of the Isles. The region was rather complex as in 1098, King Edgar of Scotland had ceded the western seaboard to King Magnus 'Barelegs' of Norway, but Somerled's son Dougall (who started the MacDougall clan), and two of Somerled's nephews, Donald, (who started the MacDonald clan), and Rory, (who started the MacRuari clan) all held significant power. These 3 clans in time started their own fighting and power struggles between each other, whilst none accepted either Norwegian or Scottish sovereignty, although Duncan's son, Ewan MacDougall, the new King of the Isles, latterly supported the Norwegian monarch and fought against the Scottish King Alexander II. The relationship between the Kings of Scotland and Norway deteriorated until matters were finally brought to a head at the Battle of Largs in 1263, a decisive victory for King Alexander III which returned the complete western seaboard solely back to Scottish rule after some 250 years. Ewan, now having also lost his King of the Isles title to the more powerful MacDonalds, and being no fool, ultimately was forced to support the King of Scots, and by marrying his children into prominent families enhanced his position and wealth which enabled him to build the great corner towers at Dunstaffnage. These family ties resulted in obligatory support for John Balliol as the King of Scots putting the MacDougalls directly against the rival Robert the Bruce who seized the Scottish throne in 1306. After Balliol was dumped, the Bruce not only had England's King Edward I (Hammer of the Scots) as an opponent, but many within Scotland including the powerful MacDougalls who had accepted Edward's rule, and were prepared to fight the Bruce. In 1306, Lame John MacDougall, Lord of Lorn, won the Battle of Dail Righ against the new King, destroying most his army and almost capturing the Bruce. Determined to subdue all rebels, as he perceived them, the Bruce took his revenge, and in 1308 at the Battle of Brander Pass, he soundly defeated Lame John MacDougall's army of some 2,000. Lame John, who had watched the battle from a galley in the loch sought refuge in his castle at Dunstaffnage, which was promptly besieged by the Bruce's army. Lame John sought reinforcements from King Edward II claiming that he had only 800 men left against Bruce's 15,000, and that none of his neighbouring clans (many no friends of the MacDougalls anyway) were coming to his aid. No English support came either, and Lame John, and his old father, Sir Alexander MacDougall surrendered Dunstaffnage and became exiles in England. Dunstaffnage, the ancestral seat of the MacDougalls then become the property of the King of Scots and remained Crown property under control of the Stewarts for 150 years. In 1431, King James I captured and hanged 300 rebel Islesmen at Dunstaffnage, the remnants of a MacDonald army who had defeated his royalist troops at the first Battle of Inverlochy where under command of a cousin of the Lord of the Isles they had killed 900 of the Earl of Mar's royalist army, loosing only 30 of their own clansmen. After their victory the MacDonalds brutally savaged the lands of Clan Cameron and Clan Chattan as vengeance for their support of the King. Much displeased by all this James I personally led an army into the Highlands to sort out (again) the problems with those damned Lords of the Isles. Prior to this the King had imprisoned the Lord of the Isles so bad blood as always was at boiling point between the royal Stewarts and the MacDonalds.

The MacDougall clan of course was still in the area and tensions between that clan and the Stewart keepers of Dunstaffnage never subdued. In 1463, Sir John Stewart of Lorn had argued with Alan MacDougall. On the day of his marriage and walking the short distance from the castle to the chapel, Stewart and his entourage were attacked by a group of MacDougalls. Stewart was fatally stabbed, dying in the chapel immediately after his marriage vows, whilst MacDougall captured the castle. It was later recaptured by royalist troops despatched by King James III, and the MacDougalls were suitably dealt with. James III granted Dunstaffnage and the lands to Colin Campbell, 1st Earl of Argyll, as the Campbells had been loyal to the Crown since fighting for the Bruce, who had installed Arthur Campbell as keeper of Dunstaffnage after ousting the MacDougalls in 1308. The power of the Campbells would be seen to increase over the centuries.

Thereafter, Dunstaffnage was used as a military base to suppress rebellious Islesmen, more often than not those bloody troublesome MacDonalds. In 1644, the Campbell Covenanter garrison held out against the Marquis of Montrose's royalist army, and in 1647 they captured Montrose's deputy, Sir Alexander MacDonald, and hanged him from the castle battlements. In 1685, the 9th Campbell Earl of Argyll was involved in a failed uprising against the new monarch, James VII, brother of Charles II, resulting in the execution of the Earl, and the royalist army setting Dunstaffnage on fire. Only 4 years later in 1688, King James was deposed and fled Scotland away to France, and the castle was returned back into Campbell hands. By all accounts this almost unheard of monarch didn't amount to much and after abandoning his Irish supporters who had risked much for him in Ireland, he was known as Seamus an Chaca meaning James the Shit.

In 1746 the castle prison held the rather cute (judging by her portraits) 24 year old Flora MacDonald a captive for her assistance in Prince Charles Edward Stewart's (Bonnie Prince Charlie) escape from Benbecula after the disastrous Battle of Culloden which forever ended the Jacobite dream. She apparently disguised the Prince as a girl to avoid recognition, discovery, and his arrest by the redcoats. Who the hell would have noticed the difference anyway?

Dunstaffnage thereafter remained in Campbell hands until 1958 when the Campbell Duke of Argyll entrusted it into government care as a monument. Even today most of the existing castle is over 700 years old, and indeed it is a fine tribute to the skills of the stone masons and builders involved.

Aug 2013

DUNVEGAN CASTLE

Dunvegan Castle on the Isle of Skye has secured the longest continual period of occupancy by the same family in the British Isles, and one of the longest in the world. The Clan Chiefs of MacLeod have owned, and resided at Dunvegan for 800 years, covering over 30 successive generations of clan chiefs. Equally surprising is that it is most likely the only castle in Scotland which has never had a change of owner or occupier in times of both peace and war, hence it's history is relatively unexciting compared to many castles in Scotland. In the early 13th century a curtain wall was erected around the hill on which previously stood a Norse fort, the only access being through a sea gate. Later circa 1350, the castle keep was built within the wall by one Malcolm MacLeod, and the tower was built in the 1500s. Over the centuries there have been numerous extensions and modifications most constructed to enhance its defensive position. The tower, however, has the rather unfortunate name of the Fairy Tower which is a bit strange for a fortress of such strength. At times surely those wild hairy MacLeod islesmen must have suggested to their boss "Er, Chief, think maybe you could change the name to the Tower of Terror. Those bloody MacDonalds are really taking the piss and we're fed up with MacFairy jibes about our dress sense going into battle"

The MacLeods supported the hero King Robert the Bruce in the Wars of Independence, but latterly fought against the royalist cause for their (on occasion) ally Donald MacDonald, Lord of the Isles against the nobles of north east Scotland at the Battle of Harlaw in Aberdeenshire in 1411. The cause of the problem was a dispute between Donald, the Lord of the Isles, and his distanced uncle Robert Stewart, Duke of Albany over ownership of the Earldom of Ross, both men claiming their right to the territory through strategic marriages, so sod all to do with loving the wife. The battle was somewhat indecisive but after the loss of some 900 clansmen, the Lord of the Isles withdrew back to his Isles. Sir Alexander Stewart, Earl of Mar, and son of the notorious Alexander Stewart, Wolf of Badenoch, (see Lochindorb Castle) had commanded the much smaller north eastern army on orders from the Duke of Albany. At the height of the fighting, the Earl had lost the majority of his men along with most of his loyal captains and knights, and believed defeat and his own death were inevitable and awaited him on the morn. When the early morning mist slowly cleared off the hill which the remaining dwindling defenders had occupied, the surrounding area was deserted other than the dead and mortally wounded still lying where they fell. MacDonald and his hordes had left under cover of night, even though he had arrived with over 10,000 hostile clansmen against the Earl of Mar's hastily put together army of just 2,500 men. The Lord of the Isles had been in league with King Henry IV of England and his real intention was to drive south into central Scotland, dispose of his uncle and take the throne of Scotland for himself, whilst English armies would pour over the border to destroy Scotland's southern forces commanded by the Duke of Albany. Somewhere along the line it all went horribly wrong. It is quite likely that the Lord of the Isles did not anticipate such opposition so early on in the venture, unsure of Mar's true strength and size of his army. The English did not invade either, most probably as Henry had hoped that both the Scots armies would annihilate themselves, and he could easily succeed where his Plantagenet forebears (Edward I, Edward II, Edward III, et al) had all failed, by taking the crown of Scotland for himself. Much blood soaked into the soil of Harlaw that day, a battle fought between 2 great-great-grandsons of Robert the Bruce. As was so tragically the norm for many centuries, Scot v Scot. King James V was invited for a banquet at MacLeod's Tables in 1540, and found himself trekking up a couple of flat topped hills for his dinner. Yup, the MacLeods liked a bit of al fresco, and thus had suitably named the local hills after themselves.

The MacLeods were staunch supporters of Charles II, King of Scots, who was attempting to gain for himself the same title for England, following in his father's footsteps albeit not all the way up to the scaffold. At the Battle of Worcester in 1651 which was a disastrous defeat for the King, with some 3,000 royalists killed and 10,000 taken prisoner, Oliver Cromwell's casualties were a mere 200. The royalist MacLeods lost over 700 clansmen in the fighting, and Charles fled, hiding in an oak tree (so they say) from Cromwell's patrols. As the death toll on the MacLeods fighting manpower was so catastrophic, and time was needed to breed new warriors, (so some pressure clearly put on the MacLeod womenfolk), the clan was 'excused from class' for the Jacobite rebellions in 1689 and 1715 (that's a whole 26 years so it would appear the female MacLeods were prone to headaches). In the 1745 Rising the Chief of the MacLeods informed Bonnie Prince Charlie (a right royal pratt in truth) that the clan would not support him in the fighting unless significant French troops arrived, which had been promised by the King of France, but which so typically with the French did not materialise. Historically the French promised much to Scotland but delivered little. The Auld Alliance which some Scots but few French bang on about is actually a bit one sided as a hell of a lot more Scots died on French soil fighting the English, than the pitifully few French who died over here fighting with the Scots against the English. Looking at the final outcome for the Jacobite cause, the MacLeod Chief's reluctance to support the prince was well justified as he lost many clansmen that fateful day on Culloden Moor (see Battle of Culloden).

The 25th Clan Chief of MacLeod was indeed a fine gentleman. In 1847 there was a potato famine (that means no Walkers crisps and chips), and poverty and starvation were rife throughout Scotland. Whilst many other land owners used this unfortunate situation to clear their lands of their undesirable non paying tenants, MacLeod was somewhat more sympathetic about his poorly folk. He ended up bankrupt providing for his tenants, renting out Dunvegan Castle for income, and to pay his way he even took employment as a lowly clerk (probably with Royal Bank of Scotland, which is indeed about as lowly as one could get). He was indeed an old fellow when he could finally afford to return to his ancestral seat.

Dunvegan Castle

June 1992

EDINBURGH CASTLE

To summarise the history of one of the most famous castles in the world on two pages is indeed an impossible task so without wasting any more words and space, here goes. The massive sprawling fortress in the centre of Edinburgh which completely dominates the extinct volcanic plug, some 350 million years old, (the volcano that is, not the castle) dates back almost 1,000 years, (the castle that is, not the volcano), but there was a fortification here long before then. Indeed there was a fort on the rock centuries before and during the Roman occupation. The Votadini tribe moved from Traprain Law (see Hailes Castle) in East Lothian to build a fort on Din Eidyn (now Edinburgh) circa AD 400 and since then this has been at the heart of Scotland's turbulent history. With so much of that history to cover, the easy option is to throw in a bunch of important diary entries which are relevant to Edinburgh Castle, from hence to save space informally referred to as E.C.

SIEGES & CAPTURES

May 1296 .... Edward I of England captures E.C. after five day siege

During 1300 .... E.C. reinforced and strengthened by Edward I following attempts by Scots to recapture

March 1314 .... Scots recapture E.C. from English on night raid during siege by Sir Thomas Randolph, Earl of Moray, and 30 picked men who scaled the rock face

During 1335 .... E.C. recaptured by English under Edward III

June 1337 .... E.C. under siege by Scots army but forced to retreat due to English relief column

April 1341 .... E.C. recaptured by the Scots under Sir William Douglas who killed English garrison of 100 men

March 1384 .... E.C. attacked but not captured by English army under Duke of Lancaster

July 1385 .... E.C. attacked but not captured by English army under Richard II

During 1400 .... E.C under siege but not captured by English army under Henry IV

August 1483 .... E.C. under siege but not captured by English army under Duke of Gloucester

October 1571........ E.C. under siege for 1 week by rival Scots. E.C. held for Mary Queen of Scots by Sir William Kirkcaldy against the Regent, John, Earl of Mar

May 1573 .... E.C. under siege for 2 years by rival Scots. E.C. lost for Mary Queen of Scots by Sir William Kirkcaldy and captured by supporters of her child, James VI

March 1639 .... E.C. captured from the royalist garrison by a Scots Covenanter army under General Alexander Leslie after short siege

September 1640 ... E.C. having been returned to the royalists under 'Peace of Berwick' treaty was yet again besieged for 3 months and captured by government troops

September 1648 ... E.C. under siege and captured by rival Scots

December 1650..... E.C. under siege for 3 months by Oliver Cromwell's army. Surrendered to Cromwell by Earl of Dundas on Christmas Eve

June 1689 .... E.C. under siege for 3 months by 7,000 troops after James VII was deposed. Duke of Gordon with 160 men surrendered when supplies ran out

September 1715 ... E.C. almost captured by 100 Jacobite Highlanders but caught scaling the rock face and defeated

September 1745 ... E.C. remained in Hanoverian control although the Jacobites took control of Edinburgh at beginning of final Jacobite rising

August 2019 .... E.C. under siege from Chinese and American tourists

The oldest part of the existing castle is St. Margaret's Chapel which was built by her son David I circa 1150 and the newest section is additional barracks for the garrison in 1796. These days Edinburgh Castle caters for some 1.5 million visitors every year, and the world famous Military Tattoo is performed during the Edinburgh Festival every August (excluding nasty virus years).

1081.................... Edinburgh Rock decided as best location for castle by Malcolm II to govern his kingdom, and thus the start of Edinburgh Castle as seat of power for monarchs

1440.................... 'The Black Dinner'. The murder of young 6th Earl of Douglas and his brother to reduce the powerful House of Douglas

1514.................... New artillery defences built following massive defeat of Scots army at Battle of Flodden in 1513. Also Flodden Wall built

1633.................... Charles I stays night before his coronation. The last reigning monarch ever to stay in E.C.

1651.................... Oliver Cromwell strengthens defences after capture of E.C.

1720s .... On recommendation from Hanoverian General Wade, new artillery bastions and batteries built to defend against Jacobite attacks

1756-1815 .... Castle vaults used as mass prisons for PoW's from Seven Years War (1756-1763), American Wars of Independence (1775-1783), and Napoleonic Wars (1803-1815)

1923.................... Disbandment after 263 years of permanent full time garrison at E.C. instigated by Charles II in 1660

Oct 1993

EILEAN DONAN CASTLE

Donan was a 7th century Celtic saint who had settled as a hermit on a small islet just off the shores of Loch Duish, on the road to the Isle of Skye, hence the name, Eilean Donan (Isle of Donan), although he met his fate elsewhere on the island of Eigg in AD 618 executed by pagans, who had kindly consented to let him say his last prayers before they hacked his head off. So it would appear that the saintly Donan did not quite succeed in converting these fellows.

There had been a fortification here since the Iron Age, so likely some 2,000 years ago. Much later in the 13th century circa 1240 the original castle was built by King Alexander II for defence against the constant Viking invasions. His son, the warrior King Alexander III, finally rid Scotland of the Norsemen forever at the Battle of Largs in 1263 and it is claimed that the King gave Eilean Donan to a favoured clansman Colin Mackenzie as just reward for disposing of so many Vikings, ie, killing them. In 1306, the Mackenzies gave shelter to Robert the Bruce at Eilean Donan after his defeat by Lame John MacDougall, Lord of Lorn at the Battle of Dail Righ. Two years later, the Bruce would turn the cards when he soundly defeated Lame John at the Battle of Brander Pass in 1308 thus destroying the MacDougall dominance in Argyll (see Dunstaffnage Castle).

Serious feuding came about between the Mackenzies and the MacDonalds over ownership of Eilean Donan, something which was hardly unusual in the west with all them unruly clans roaming about. The MacDonalds were somewhat of the opinion that the whole region was theirs to rule by right, and to a point so it was, as records show that in the 14th century the castle was dramatically extended and strengthened by the Earl of Ross, one of the feared MacDonald Lords of the Isles. For long the castle was involved in warfare between rival clans and changed hands numerous times. In one incident in 1539, the powerful rebel Donald Gorm MacDonald, Lord of Sleat attacked the castle with a fleet of 50 MacDonald warships. The occupying royalist garrison of MacRaes, who held the castle on behalf of the Mackenzies (who were back in there again) was severely outnumbered and just prior to Gorm's hordes of Islesmen capturing the castle, one Duncan MacRae of Kintail, leader of the dwindling defenders shot his last barbed arrow at Gorm, who was directing operations from one of his galleys. MacRae cursed when he missed the rebel's chest, at which he was aiming, but instead the arrow had severed an artery in Gorm's foot. With their Lord of Sleat bleeding to death, and without any forthcoming commands from any other, the remaining attackers abandoned the onslaught and retreated back up the loch.

During the 1719 Jacobite rising, Spain was also involved in attempts to restore the Royal House of Stewart, and William Mackenzie, 5th Earl of Seaforth despatched 300 Spanish soldiers to garrison Eilean Donan. The attempt was rather short lived as 3 English naval frigates arrived soon after and with somewhat more success than Donald Gorm's fleet, they bombarded Eilean Donan beyond recognition, and likely the Spaniards inside beyond any recognition as well. Just to make sure they hadn't missed anything, the English then blew up the inside of the castle with barrels of gunpowder. After the failure of the rising, the 5th Earl was forfeit and lost all his lands and titles albeit not his head. It remained a total ruin until the early 20th century when John MacRae-Gilstrap proceeded with the most remarkable of restorations re-creating Eilean Donan. The castle was recently rebuilt and to this day the MacRaes have remained as constables thereof.

As Eilean Donan is one of the most photographed castles in UK, almost everyone will surely at one time or another have had a photo of this castle hanging on their kitchen wall on that glossy calendar sent every Christmas from some old relative in Scarborough. If there are purple flowers and butterflies on the wall, it will be June or July, and if it's snowy with a robin, it will be December. If there is just a nail, the bloody calendar has fallen on the floor again.

EILEAN DONAN CASTLE - AMC 8.8.93

Aug 1993

FENTON TOWER

Built a few miles from North Berwick in East Lothian, circa 1550, the 4 storey Fenton tower house was improved in 1587 by Sir John Carmichael, Warden of the Scottish West March (even though East Lothian is of course on the East March). Wardens of the Marches were sort of early type police chiefs responsible for law and order, and national security on each nation's borderlands, so not exactly a part time occupation when considering the relationship between Scotland and England over the centuries. Sir John Carmichael had in 1575 seriously disagreed over some matter with his counterpart, the English Warden, Sir John Forster at a meeting on the border at Carter Bar (close to where the burger van is now parked up on the A68 road) resulting in a small battle in which Carmichael's men killed quite a few English soldiers and captured the English leadership, which in turn proved to be somewhat embarrassing for the Scottish Parliament as this incident occurred during one of those rare periods of total peace between the two nations. Sir John Carmichael, however, was held in very high regard by his English counterparts, and on occasion personally escorted Scottish offenders to the English Warden for justice at the formidable English border fortress, Carlisle Castle. Most of the English March Wardens greatly respected him (albeit the exception would likely have been Sir John Forster), and the Bishop of Durham referred to him as "the most expert borderer". Whilst proving himself very fair and judicial to both sides, he was also well favoured by Queen Elizabeth I of England and her parliament, which in turn made him an enemy to not a few in Scotland. He was an excellent soldier and captain of mercenaries and had proved himself highly efficient in border control as the Keeper of Liddesdale, when he was captain of Hermitage Castle where over the centuries many evil and foul deeds occurred (see Hermitage Castle). Sir John Carmichael was murdered but ironically by Scots rather than English, when in 1600 he was ambushed by a gang of some 14 Armstrongs on his way to a Warden's court at Langholm in the borders, Carmichael having persecuted them following their constant reiving (cattle stealing) activities and no doubt other bad deeds. The gang of assassins, high on their successful murder, thereafter ventured into England to steal horses, and whilst there they created much havoc. Both countries were now keen to arrest the culprits. Sir John's brother, Carmichael of Edrom, apprehended two of the Armstrong ring leaders, Tom Armstrong and Adam 'The Pecket', and after their trial in Edinburgh in 1601, these two were sentenced, and had their right arms chopped off, following which they were then hanged, with their remains left to rot on gibbets on Edinburgh's Burghmuir. Years later the rest of the outlaws were still being pursued for Sir John's murder, and in 1605 one Sandie Armstrong was also convicted and hanged. It is interesting to learn that the Armstrongs planned the murder at a football match so it certainly proves that thugs attending football matches are not confined to modern times as this foul deed occurred more than 420 years ago. The Armstrongs were the most formidable and feared border family involved in reiving on an industrial scale, frequent killing, and constant cross border mischief, with little doubt doing more damage on forays in both Scotland and England than any other border family ever could, which was quite a claim. Circa 1528 the unruly Armstrongs could put 3,000 men into the saddle, and that's a hell of a lot of trouble. In 1530 James V under pressure from other border lords took troops down in person, met and hanged the powerful self ruling and law making border chieftain Johnnie Armstrong and 36 of his personal tail and bodyguard of well armed gentlemen.

In 1591, King James VI of Scotland had been provided protection in Fenton Tower by Sir John Carmichael following the King's defeat and his escape from an opposing Scottish army in Fife, and his obvious need for safe hiding having hastily sailed over the Firth of Forth. After Sir John Carmichael's murder, James VI granted Fenton to Sir Thomas Erskine in 1603, the year of the Union of the Crowns between Scotland and England, and later in 1631 it came under the ownership of Sir John Maxwell who in 1646 became the Earl of Dirleton. Such ownership became Fenton's downfall as after Oliver Cromwell's army had invaded Scotland in 1650, and having much bombarded the nearby Dirleton Castle (see Dirleton Castle) the English went to the next-on-the-hit-list and soon rendered the much smaller Fenton Tower into a similar condition, after which it remained in it's ruinous state until very recently. In the early 2000s the farmer/owner of the ruin renovated Fenton at very great cost, and it is now a luxury tower house for short term rental and accommodation, chef and wine cellar included, also at very great cost.

AMC - 1983

FENTON TOWER
AMC 10-7-05

July 2005 (Carmichael crest, 1983)

CASTLE GLOOM (alias CASTLE CAMPBELL)

Situated in lofty isolation in the Ochils hills in Central Scotland between the deep ravines and gushing waters over the rocks of the aptly named "Burn of Care" and the "Burn of Sorrow", Castle Gloom was originally held by the Stewarts before passing to the Campbells by marriage in the late 1400s. Gloom was used by Colin Campbell, 1st Earl of Argyll, and for centuries thereafter was used by the successive Campbell Earls of Argyll as their principal lowland stronghold. Their power base and most of their lands were through in the west in Argyll, where the ancestral seat of the Chiefs of Clan Campbell always was and still is as at Inveraray Castle, albeit these days such is not the original castle, although the site of that rockery is close to the new mansion. However, due to the increasing political clout of the Campbells, they clearly believed they needed a substantial domicile within easy reach of the powerful lowland nobles, and also of course the monarch who always apparently needed advice and who tended to reside at the nearby Stirling Castle.

Castle Gloom dates back to 15th century and was so called Gloom as rather a lot of nasty things are said to have happened there. Whilst the Campbells were not adverse to nasty things, more often than not being the perpetrators of such, the 1st Campbell Earl of Argyll's spin doctors and marketing gurus suggested a change of name would improve the image of the place, and after much, or seemingly minimal deliberation, the name Castle Campbell was decided upon. However, even in them days bureaucracy prevailed, and it required an Act of Parliament in 1490 to sanction the change. Gloom of course sounds much better.

In 1645, the castle was largely destroyed and burned by the Campbell hating MacLeans from the Isle of Mull, who formed part of James Graham, 1st Marquis of Montrose's royalist army fighting for the cause of King Charles I, (well before his head was lopped off by the English Parliamentarians in 1649) whilst the Campbells were staunch supporters of the extremist Covenanters. It is quite likely that the attack on Castle Campbell was more to do with the long running MacLean feud against the Campbells than for any sound military reason. Much of Montrose's army was made up Highland clans and Islesmen, and whilst they were formidable and fearsome fighters, they had a rather bad habit of disappearing from the royalist army on personal ventures of revenge and obligatory destruction. Archibald Campbell, 8th Earl of Argyll loathed Montrose with a vengeance largely on account of Montrose switching sides from the Covenanter cause to the royalist cause and as a result of this, the series of battles Montrose had then won against the Covenanter armies, not infrequently involving Campbell troops. At the second Battle of Inverlochy in 1645 for instance, Montrose's army of 1,500 destroyed a Campbell army of 3,000 when Montrose and Alastair MacColla MacDonald launched a dawn attack against the somewhat surprised Campbell army who had believed Montrose's army to be 30 miles further north. The Campbells had been pursuing the royalist army with the plan to annihilate it with the support of a second larger Covenanter army under the Earl of Seaforth travelling from Inverness. In what is regarded as one of the greatest flanking strategies in British history, Montrose force marched his army through the cold night over some of the wildest and toughest terrain in Scotland traversing Ben Nevis and then attacked with a long single line only 2 men deep to avoid being outflanked. The 8th Earl of Argyll slunk off to hide in his galley on the loch leaving the command to his general, Duncan Campbell of Auchinbreck who was killed in the action along with 1,500 Campbells whereas Montrose lost only 250 men. Not unlike the occasion of the MacLeans attacking Castle Campbell, it is widely regarded that MacColla's involvement was much more about the MacDonald v Campbell feud than any interest in the cause for King Charles I. A demoralised and cowardly Argyll sailed off in his galley. The Campbell got his satisfaction, however, when the royalist's most able and loyal general was taken from them, in 1650. The Great Montrose as he was also known, was captured after the Battle of Carbisdale, when he was betrayed ironically by a MacLeod with whom he had trusted and sought safe shelter. A fatal mistake unfortunately. Thereafter, the 37 year old noble was maltreated and taken to Edinburgh dressed in rags and mounted on a scrawny pony destined for the knackers yard. He was sentenced to death by

Campbell and the Covenanters before he ever arrived in the city, and with minimal delay he was hanged near St Giles Cathedral in Edinburgh, as a traitor, which of course was ridiculous as he was more loyal than any of the extremists who had sentenced him, including the Campbell. The Covenanters were not yet done. Montrose was dismembered and his head was stuck on a spike for all to see and it remained there for 11 years. The ultimate shame was that shortly after his execution, Campbell and the Covenanter government switched their allegiances to support King Charles II, for whom Montrose had sacrificed so much including ultimately his own life. Montrose was regarded as the most handsome man in Scotland, whilst descriptions and paintings of Campbell indicate he was quite an ugly twisted ogre, probably added to the Earl's hatred and jealousy of the Marquis. Old portraits of the time painted of both men indicate they didn't exactly look like twins.

The happy, or rather should we say justified, conclusion to this sorry part of Scottish history comes some years later. In 1661 the new Scots Parliament revoked all sentences passed on the late Great Montrose and the largest state funeral ever seen in Scotland was held the next year. The organisers had to delay the funeral for some time to collect all of Montrose's body parts from various cities and towns where his disintegrated limbs had been put on spikes in prominent places. The great general was finally laid to rest in St. Giles Cathedral. Meanwhile the Campbell 8th Earl of Argyll was arrested, held in prison in Edinburgh Castle and soon after was executed for treason, his head being stuck on the same spike, which for 11 years had held a much nobler head.

Castle Gloom was again in need of a new lord.

Aug 1993

HAILES CASTLE & TRAPRAIN LAW

Built in the shadow of Traprain Law, it was actually a Northumbrian Lord, Sir Hugo de Gourlay who built Hailes Castle in the 1290s, as although he was English, it was not uncommon for English nobles at the time, to hold lands in Scotland, just as many Scottish nobles held lands in England. The timing for Sir Hugo, however, was a tad unfortunate though, as the castle was built only a few years before the Wars of Independence and as the de Gourlays understandably supported their Liege Lord Edward I and thus the English invaders, they in turn lost Hailes and their lands which were forfeited by the Scottish Crown, after Robert the Bruce took control of Scotland. The castle and lands then passed to the Hepburns who extended the castle and added the huge 4 storey tower. At that time the Hepburns were vassals of the Earls of Dunbar and March but bitterness and hatred would soon develop between these two families.

In 1400 the garrison at Hailes successfully withstood a siege by an English army under the command of Sir Henry Percy, nicknamed Hotspur, although the end of the siege was hastened by a surprise night attack from a Scottish army under Archibald, Master of Douglas (later 4th Earl), who intent on capturing such a prize as Hotspur for ransom, pursued the English as far as the border being some 50 miles away, so determined was the Douglas. The feuding between the two powerful border families of the Douglases on the Scottish side, and the Percys on the Northumbrian side had been going on for some 100 years (see Tantallon Castle). Hotspur left groups of archers behind to slow down the pursuing Scots and safely fled over the border. In 1443 Hailes Castle fell to the English supporting turncoat Archibald Dunbar who mercilessly slaughtered the entire Hepburn garrison more out of hatred more than for any sound military reason. The Dunbars were justifiably loathed by most Scots as they were considered untrustworthy and treasonable due to their continual bad habits of supporting the English. On account of this the title of Earl of Dunbar lay dormant until 1605 when it was resurrected for George Home, 1st Lord of Berwick.

Hailes was bombarded by Cromwell's artillery immediately after his great victory against the Scots army under the command of Sir David Leslie at the Battle of Dunbar in 1650, which ended the castle's history as a fortification, other than as a garrison for Cromwell's soldiers. At the battle a few miles from Hailes some 3,000 Scots were killed (according to Cromwell), whereas Cromwell lost only 20 men (according to Cromwell) from his army of 9,000. Some might call that a decisive result, others may well dispute those exaggerated figures. Leslie, an extremely capable general with many victories under his belt (including defeating the Marquis of Montrose at the Battle of Carbisdale in 1650), was, however, much disadvantaged as he was forced to take his orders from the crazy zealots of the Church of Scotland who were controlling the Scottish Parliament and to such tragic end also the Scots army. These fanatical lunatics cost Scotland very dearly on that September day. In the aftermath of the battle while the Scottish soldiery was still being chased and butchered, it is to be hoped that more than a few of the crazed ministers likewise met their maker. The castle was lastly owned by Arthur Balfour, 1st Earl of Balfour who was British Prime Minister from 1902-1905, and had been born only a few miles from Hailes in 1848. He donated Hailes to government care as a monument in 1926. Whilst obviously ruinous, much remains of the impressive structure and vaults.

The history of TRAPRAIN LAW is somewhat older than Hailes as it is a hill 220 metres (720 ft) high, but it's relatively flat top was for centuries used as an ancient town which could be well defended against attackers. How old is not exactly known, but there is evidence of a burial ground 1500 BC and fort ramparts 1000 BC, and over the centuries the ramparts around the hill top were replaced and repositioned several times. In the 1st century AD the Romans referred to a tribe called the Votadini whose principal settlement was on this hill, until they relocated their capital to the volcanic rock which now accommodates Edinburgh Castle. The Votadini tribe occupied the hill for some 600 years and during the relatively short time the Romans settled in Caledonia (what them Romans called today's Scotland) they looked on this tribe as allies, as most likely both of these extremely different cultures found it mutually beneficial to maintain this prosperous arable area and jointly fend off undesirable invaders.

The region Lothian is named after the 6th century pagan King Loth who circa AD 525 had his daughter Teneu thrown over the cliff face side of Traprain Law after sentencing her to death when he found out she was pregnant albeit raped by the Welsh Prince Owan mab Urien and had refused to marry him. Not a Loth of sympathy from an understanding dad then. The Princess survived the fall and she was found alive by local folk who in order to save her from further execution attempts by her father, set her adrift in a coracle (tiny round boat) on the Firth of Forth. On the other side she was given shelter at Culross in Fife by Saint Serf and his community and whilst there she gave birth to a boy, she called Mungo, meaning 'very dear one'. Time would show Saint Mungo to be a great religious figure. Aged 25 he set up a community on the River Clyde and was thus the founder of the city of Glasgow, dying there in AD 614. Glasgow of course always has been and still is in need of missionaries. The legacy of King Loth lives on 1,500 years later emblazoned for decades on thousands of Lothian's maroon and white double-decker buses and indeed King Loth himself (due to his age) would qualify for a free bus (or chariot) pass. Teneu is regarded as Scotland's first ever historically recorded rape victim, battered woman, and unmarried mother. There have been more than a few since.

Sept 2013

HERMITAGE CASTLE

A most forbidding fortress of well justified evil reputation, Hermitage Castle dominates its bleak location in the Scottish border country. It was once referred to as 'The guardhouse of the bloodiest valley in Britain'. The castle was first built circa 1240 by Sir Nicholas de Soulis and it's proximity to the English border so enraged King Henry II of England, that he threatened invasion. Years later when Henry III heard the castle was being fortified, he also planned for war, such was the strategic importance of this place. De Soulis, a huge horrendous beast of a man with bad breath always dressed in black with a red cap, and was heavily into the black arts, devil worship and had a bad habit of abducting children. After killing them in many nasty ways he used their little body parts for various concoctions and evil sorcery. Generally, one could say he was not considered a decent bloke. In fact he was a right real bastard. At some point his own garrison and the local folk, fearing and tiring of his foul deeds, and with an increasing shortage of kids in the area, apprehended him, wrapped him in lead, and boiled him alive in a brass cauldron at a nearby stone circle known as Nine Staine Rig. They boiled the tyrant until his flesh slipped off his bones, and his bones then melted. The de Soulis family lost Hermitage in 1320 after the involvement of William de Soulis in a plan to assassinate King Robert the Bruce, as de Soulis also claimed he had a justifiable, albeit very, very remote claim to the throne. His attempt was, somewhat unsuccessful as he ended up incarcerated in Dumbarton Castle.

Due to it's border location, for centuries Hermitage endured recurrent occupation by both Scottish and English garrisons during the lengthy Wars of Independence and for some 200 years Hermitage was one of the powerful Douglas family strongholds. In 1338 some years after the Bruce's death, one Sir William Douglas, Knight of Liddlesdale and illegitimate son of the Black Douglas, (the Bruce's best friend and one of his ablest commanders) besieged Hermitage and captured it from the English under the command of Sir Ralph de Neville, thereafter securing it as Douglas property. Soon afterwards, this Douglas acted most strangely and quite like a schizophrenic. He imprisoned in Hermitage his former best friend and fellow warrior, Sir Alexander Ramsay of Dalwolsey (Lord of Dalhousie Castle) with whom he had fought the English at many a battle, and the two were the most renowned knights in Scotland. Ramsay had attacked and ousted the English from the royal castle of Roxburgh and as a reward, the Bruce's son, the young but naive David II, had made Ramsay, Sheriff of Teviotdale which he desired not, as such was a position already held by his friend Sir William Douglas, also titled the Flower of Chivalry, for his abilities as a knight. Douglas was incensed as he already controlled the West March from Hermitage Castle, and without warning he launched an armed attack against Ramsay, taking him into custody at Hermitage (see Dalhousie Castle). Sir Alexander was starved to death in a dungeon there, although he kept himself alive for 17 days feeding on a trickle of grain leaking from the granary above. Some years later in 1353, Sir William Douglas, was ambushed and murdered by his own nephew, godson and namesake, William, 1st Earl of Douglas, as the Flower of Chivalry had quite disgraced the noble reputation of Douglas. Such ensured Hermitage remained in Douglas hands, albeit different Douglas hands. By 1455, James II had totally subdued the rebellious Black Douglas, Earls of Douglas, and Hermitage was passed to the Red Douglas, Earls of Angus. However, the Crown was to later find out that their problems with those Douglases were far from over (see Tantallon Castle).

In 1492 the young but very able King James IV, concerned over Red Douglas loyalty to the Scottish crown, ordered Archibald Douglas, 5th Earl of Angus to exchange his Hermitage Castle with the Earl of Bothwell, for Bothwell Castle near Glasgow in Lanarkshire, as the King was concerned about leaving such a strategic border fortress as Hermitage in the hands of potential Douglas rebels. It thus passed to the Hepburns. Who got the best deal out of this swap, I really don't know.

In 1566 Mary Queen of Scots visited Hermitage to see her lover, James Hepburn, 4th Earl of Bothwell, who had been badly wounded in a border skirmish with some cattle reivers (quite possibly Armstrongs) and he was recovering there. Mary however, did not stay the night, and it is almost certain that Bothwell did not get his royal oats, (not even a trickle). She would, however, marry him the next year (see Borthwick Castle).

In 1573, the castle came under the control of Sir John Carmichael, Warden of the Middle March, and despite being renowned as one of the most able wardens ever appointed, he was murdered by Armstrongs in 1600 (see Fenton Tower). The last Earl of Bothwell died in Italy in 1624, bankrupt and disgraced (what a way to go), and all his lands and properties passed to the Scotts of Buccleuch. Hermitage was abandoned in the 17th century as it lacked any artillery defences, so it was spared the brutal bombardment of Cromwell's Parliamentarian cannons, which had devastated so many other Scottish castles, and for that matter more than a few English ones.

Hermitage still stands very much intact structurally, although somewhat ruinous on the inside, and can be visited by those who are able to locate this gloomy and rather terrifying fortress in its bleak and lonely Scottish border country domain. It really is a brutal looking place.

June 1998

INVERARAY CASTLE

This is the only castle included which is not actually a castle but a big posh house, in fact a very big posh mansion. The main reason that it is not a castle is that it has a tad too much glazing particularly at low level and thus would not score very highly in gaining defence feature points. There is nothing left of the original (proper) 4 storey 15th century castle which was located very close by but was largely destroyed by the Campbells arch enemy the Marquis of Montrose in 1644, (see Castle Gloom) so with the need for a new ancestral home for the Campbell Dukes of Argyll this new Gothic version built from 1743 was based on a classical mansion design as it seemed likely there would never be open warfare again in the land although the Battle of Culloden took place a mere 3 years later. Inveraray is not alone and Scotland has a number of so called castles like Dunrobin, Thirlestone, Drumlanrig, Floors, Culzean and of course HM Queen's holiday cottage up north at Balmoral this one built as recently as 1853. All of these are extremely impressive palaces for the landed gentry and some may retain a small part of an original castle but none of these as they stand now are real castles.

So important was the need for a perfect view from his new domicile that the Duke had the town of Inveraray demolished and rebuilt a half mile away over on the left (the local population's left or the Duke's left?). When Dr Johnson visited in 1773 he exclaimed "What I admire here is the total defiance of expense".

This grand mansion does, however, house a remarkable collection of old weaponry, general old posh furniture/tapestry/paintings stuff, and Rob Roy MacGregor's dirk (knife) and sporran (albeit not those used by Liam Neeson in that film of the same name) on display in one half of the building which is open to the public. The other half ain't.

Oct 2019   Inveraray Moon

There are several ghosts in the vicinity varying from one of Montrose's victims from the 1644 attack being an Irish harpist boy who stayed when the Duke had fled and was killed and dismembered by Montrose's Irish mercenaries as a traitor, with them discarding the boy's body parts in the Duke's bed. Also a young servant murdered by Jacobites, marching redcoat troops, and even a birlinn (Scottish galley) on Loch Fyne seen only when one of the senior Campbells is about to pop off. Some lordly killjoy Campbells deny the existence of any spooks. The place continues to be the home of the Dukes of Argyll, currently the 13th Duke, and there is quite a bit of history about the Campbells and preceding Dukes throughout the book.

The small town of Inveraray along the shores of Loch Fyne is an excellent place to visit and hole up for a few days with good shops, a fascinating law court and jail museum (see also Ballachulish Gibbet), and characteristic hotels with great food, principally The George (now run by the 7th generation of the Clark family), and also The Inveraray Inn which first opened in 1775 are both highly recommended.

Oct 2019

Seat of Mac Cailein Mór

LOCHINDORB CASTLE

Lochindorb Castle is best remembered as the lair of the Wolf of Badenoch, the unruly, evil, and uncontrollable brother of the weak and pitiful King Robert III of Scots, both men being great-grand sons of the hero King Robert the Bruce and that is where the similarity ends. Alexander Stewart, Earl of Buchan, gained his nickname The Wolf of Badenoch, from his notoriously dastardly deeds including hunting men for sport when tiring of the more boring boar, wolves, wildcats and deer etc. The Wolf, with his favoured lords and guests would patiently wait, on the edge of the vast Rothiemurchus Forest whilst his clansmen and gillies started brush fires amongst the trees. Every living thing, animal and man which fled out into the open to escape the flames, including social outcasts and caterans living and hiding in the forest were immediately impaled with hails of arrows, spears and other such missiles from these medieval sportsmen.

Prisoners at Lochindorb were incarcerated in an underground pit which always retained about a metre (3 ft) of filthy cold water above the ground, whereby any with the misfortune to partake of the Wolf's hospitality downstairs had a couple of options open to them. Either to stand in the putrid water up to the groin, or if that was not to their liking, then drowning was an option. If after several days of this, the standing victims still survived, albeit a bit damp, stiff and chilly, and depending on the Wolf's mood at the time, they may be freed. On the other hand they may be hanged.

When his other brother, Robert, Duke of Albany (see Doune Castle), who in reality governed Scotland as Regent, in lieu of the pathetic monarch, arranged the papal excommunication of the Wolf, the contempt shown by the Wolf for both his brothers and the Holy Church was in 1390, to take an army of some 2,000 clansmen to Elgin and burn down the magnificent Cathedral there along with numerous other churches and godly things. At one time the Wolf even took a strong Highland army south intent on capturing the Scottish throne from his weak brother but he was defeated by forces sent north by his brother, the Duke of Albany. The Wolf had several other castles throughout his Strathspey territories, one of these being at Ruthven, now the site of Ruthven Barracks, the imposing Hanoverian fortification (seen from A9 road) built in 1720s for repressing the Jacobites. In 1394, the Wolf and a garrison of his henchmen were at Ruthven Castle when a tall dark figure dressed totally in black arrived without warning and challenged Alexander Stewart to a game of chess, the wager being nothing other than the Stewart's soul. After a thunderous stormy night, morning revealed that every single person in the castle was dead lying in twisted contorted positions and the castle itself was totally engulfed in flames. The Devil had acquired the soul of the Wolf of Badenoch and Speyside could relax at last.

Lochindorb was originally held by the powerful Comyns, whom the Bruce had really pissed off when he murdered his fellow Guardian of Scotland, the double dealing John the 'Red Comyn', Lord of Badenoch, in a church in Dumfries in 1306. Prior to that Lochindorb had been captured by the English and visited by Edward I of England in 1303 on a whistle-stop tour of his recently conquered Scotland. Later in 1335 it was besieged by Scots under the Earl of Moray who had to withdraw under threat of a large approaching English army led by Edward III. The castle then passed to the Stewarts but was abandoned in 1455 not too long after the occupation by the Wolf, and thereafter his more well intentioned and more honourable son, also Sir Alexander Stewart who became Earl of Mar by marriage and he who won the Battle of Harlaw. Finally the lands passed to the Douglas Earls of Moray, then the Campbells of Cawdor in 1606, and lastly the Ogilvie Earls of Seafield in 1750.

Lochindorb remains in lonely isolation, miles from any other habitation, an unreachable scant ruin on that small islet. Indeed quite eerie when you find it.

April 2013

CASTLE STALKER

The Chiefs of Appin

Occupying a small rocky outcrop in Loch Laich in Argyll, the original fortification Caisteal Stalcaire (Gaelic for fortress of the hunter) was built by the MacDougall Lords of Lorn who had suffered a change of fortunes as of course did many in Scottish history. The MacDougall's principal castle had for long been the great fortress of Dunstaffnage near Oban built circa 1220, and they built Stalcaire (Stalker) some 100 years later, Ewan MacDougall, having lost his Lord of the Isles position and title to the even more hostile MacDonalds.

In 1388 Duncan Stewart of Appin, the new Lord of Lorn, built another castle at Stalker replacing the original MacDougall fortification. He was appointed Chamberlain of the Isles by King James IV for the Appin Stewarts support in crushing the powerful MacDonald Lord of the Isles, who were forever a threat to the monarchy, the MacDonalds firmly believing their somewhat expanding territory was no part of Scotland but in fact their own personal kingdom, and at times even intent on taking the throne of Scotland.

The repressed MacDougall clan was, however, with a rather bad attitude, still roaming about Argyll and the situation between them and the Stewarts always at boiling point. In 1463, the keeper of both Stalker and Dunstaffnage Castles, Sir John Stewart, the new Lord of Lorn had argued with one Alan MacDougall. On the day of Stewart's marriage and whilst walking the short distance from Dunstaffnage Castle to the chapel, Stewart and his entourage were attacked by this Alan and a group of MacDougalls. Stewart was fatally stabbed, dying in the chapel immediately after taking his vows, whilst the MacDougalls proceeded to capture the castle. The marriage albeit a somewhat short one of maybe five minutes, with no ensuing wedding piss up, jokes about the mother-in-law, and eager excuses for early to bed etc, legitimized his son Dugald Stewart in becoming the 1st Chief of Appin. Five years later in 1468 Dugald Stewart avenged his father's murder at the Battle of Stalc, directly opposite Castle Stalker on the mainland where the Stewarts including their hereditary henchmen, the Carmichaels, defeated a combined MacDougall and MacFarlane army, and during which battle, Dugald Stewart personally sought out and killed his father's murderer, Alan MacDougall.

Bad blood between the Appin Stewarts and the Campbells of Argyll really kicked off in 1520 when some Campbells murdered Sir Alexander Stewart whilst he was quietly fishing in Loch Laich very close to his Castle Stalker. This deed was avenged in 1544 by his son aged 24 whom, because of his huge size and physical strength, was known as Donald of the Hammers. He went to Dunstaffnage and killed 9 Campbells outright. In 1547 he led the Stewarts of Appin at the Battle of Pinkie, and when he died in 1607, he was buried on the nearby Isle of Lismore where his faithful henchman, a Carmichael, is also buried. In 1620 Castle Stalker changed hands from Stewart to Campbell, not as the usual result of their feud or warfare, but following a drunken wager over a game of cards in which Duncan Stewart, 7th Chief of Appin, lost by somewhat recklessly gambling his Castle Stalker against an 8 oared boat. Clearly not a dead sure bet. Later in 1689, the Stewarts seized back the castle in the name of King James VII after a lengthy siege, but lost it again to the Campbells after a rival siege the following year in 1690.

The Jacobites besieged the castle in 1745 with 300 Appin clansmen including Stewarts and Carmichaels, but they could not oust the garrison of 60 Campbell redcoats even using cannon. After the Battle of Culloden in 1746, the castle was used as a prison to incarcerate Jacobites, and a collection point where Highlanders surrendered their weapons. The last resident Campbell was born there in 1775 and the castle was occupied until the late 1700s. Circa 1840 the roof fell in and Stalker became ruinous. By means of cash rather than siege, it became a Stewart property again in 1908 when Charles Stewart bought the old ruin and in the 1960s it was fully restored. It is now used for reclusive private habitation, the waters of Loch Laich deterring even those bloody annoying funeral touting life insurance reps.

Nov 2004

TANTALLON CASTLE

Whilst Threave Castle in Galloway was the principal seat of power of the Black Douglas, the Red Douglas stronghold was Tantallon Castle in East Lothian. Indeed a most unique castle in that it was one of the most impregnable fortifications in the land but in reality the castle is only one massive wall, some 15 metres (49 ft) high and 3.5 metres (12 ft) thick built totally of red sandstone. Within and behind this single wall were the lord's halls, private quarters, barracks, guardrooms, prison, kitchens, stables, brewhouse and even gardens and orchards, protected not by typical castle walls but geology being shear cliffs dropping down to the waters of the Firth of Forth securing those sides against attack. Tantallon is in fact a chunk of headland cut off by one bloody big wall. Tantallon was built in 1350 by William, 1st Earl of Douglas, a nephew of the Good Sir James Douglas, who was one of Robert the Bruce's most able and loyal commanders, resulting in the Bruce bestowing much land and wealth to the Good Sir James, which kickstarted the Douglas powerhouse. By his royal mistress, Margaret Stewart, Countess of Angus, the 1st Earl had a son George who became Earl of Angus when only a young boy. William Douglas was succeeded by his eldest son, James. Following the untimely death of James, 2nd Earl of Douglas, who had no legitimate male heir, the Douglas family divided, the Red Douglas, becoming the Earls of Angus at Tantallon, and the title of 3rd Earl of Douglas passing to Sir Archibald Douglas, The Grim (cousin of 1st Earl of Douglas and son of the Good Sir James), in Galloway, who became the Black Douglas faction. James, 2nd Earl of Douglas, a notable warrior, was for long preoccupied with the ongoing family feud against the English Northumbrian family of the Percys, each being the prominent family on their respective side of the border. In 1388 a Scottish army of some 30,000 invaded both the West and East Marches of England to deter the English from further invasions of Scotland and bring them to the negotiating table. The 2nd Earl treated his East March foray with some 7,000 Douglases as more of an excuse to have a go at the Percys rather than any advantage for the national interest. On his return from a somewhat successful burning, pillaging, and reiving foray well into enemy territory but now with an army only half of it's original size due to mass desertion, the Douglas besieged Newcastle and goaded Sir Henry Percy, known as Hotspur, into single combat. The siege was unsuccessful and Hotspur declined the Earl's most considerate offer of personal combat, but after the Scots army departed north encumbered by their hundreds of stolen cattle, Hotspur urgently pursued the Douglases with an army of some 5,000 and attacked the Scot's camps at Otterburn during the hours of darkness. Despite the surprise attack, Douglas and John Dunbar, Earl of Moray outflanked and defeated the larger English army. Douglas was killed in the fighting, some suggesting that he was stabbed in the back by his own armour bearer on instructions from Scotland's Regent, Robert Stewart, Earl of Fife and brother of the feeble Robert III, intent on reducing the power of the Douglas (see Doune Castle). The Earl of Fife was meanwhile commanding the much larger Scots army on the West March with minimal results compared to the much smaller force in the east. Fife was ever more politician than soldier. Hotspur was captured by the Scots for ransom, this being something of an expensive embarrassment as he had a much larger force and had launched a surprise night attack on the un-expecting Scots most being asleep.

Over time clashes kicked off between the two powerful Douglas families. James, 3rd Earl of Angus used Tantallon in a vendetta against the Black Douglas, and in 1455 his brother George Douglas, later 4th Earl of Angus, led King James II's army against the Black Douglas forces at the Battle of Arkinholm. Whilst James Douglas, 9th Earl of Douglas was in England trying to muster more forces to take on James II, he had left the command to his 3 younger brothers with dire results. Archibald Douglas, Earl of Moray, was killed in the battle, Hugh Douglas, Earl of Ormonde, was captured and executed, and John Douglas, Lord of Balvenie escaped into England. Soon after, Threave Castle was captured thus putting to an end the power of the Black Douglas. The first 4 Red Douglas Earls of Angus had been quite loyal to the Crown but this changed when Archibald Douglas, 5th Earl of Angus alias 'Bell-The-Cat' entered the scene. It was now the turn of the Red Douglas to turn rebellious against their King. In 1491 the 5th Earl plotted with Henry VII of England to depose James IV resulting in the 18 year old Scottish King James attacking and besieging Tantallon with heavy artillery. The castle held out and the King realizing he could not take Tantallon by force agreed terms with Bell-The-Cat and vacated the scene. Opposing the King was fast becoming a bad habit of the Red Douglas. In 1525, Archibald, 6th Earl of Angus held the young King James V a virtual captive in Tantallon for 3 years manipulating and exercising the King's power and issuing orders for his own gain. The King escaped in 1528 and returned with a royalist army and artillery but after a 3 week siege, Tantallon again proved it could not be taken, particularly when the royalists ran out of ammunition. The Earl seeing the confusion of the retreating army and determined not to miss such an opportunity despatched 160 men from Tantallon and right under their attacker's noses, they took possession of all the best cannons and weaponry. James V ultimately took control of the castle the next year but by negotiation, and not artillery, most of which now was in Tantallon anyway.

This great fortress' final chapter was the siege by 2,000 of Oliver Cromwell's troops in 1651, when after 12 days of heavy bombardment by somewhat more effective artillery, the royalist garrison of moss troopers who had done much damage to Cromwell's lines of communication, surrendered to General Monk. Tantallon had a relatively short history of only 300 years from 1350 to 1651, but little has changed since that final bombardment, and that massive wall is still overwhelming to look at particularly when the sun so chooses to bring out the deep colour of that distinct red sandstone.

Douglas v Percy
Battle of Otterburn 1388

TANTALLON CASTLE - DMC - 11/8/93

Aug 1993 (Crests, May 1977)

Nov 2004   Castle Stalker

HEBRIDEAN HISTORY

CALLANISH STANDING STONES

The Night Watch

Erected over 5,000 years ago on the Isle of Lewis, the mysterious Callanish Standing Stones (Calanais in Gaelic) still determinedly hold the secret of their exact purpose. It is most widely believed that the Stones collectively formed a pagan Druid temple, although there are also substantial arguments that the place had great astronomical significance. The unique formation, close to the wild Atlantic coast comprises a 13 stone circle with 5 radiating avenues of stones much in the shape of a Celtic cross, but of course at this time there was no known religious significance with crosses so it dispenses with the Jesus angle. In the centre stands a 5.5 metres (18 ft) high monolith close to a Neolithic type burial cairn in which bones were once recovered. The true physical size of Callanish was not discovered until a 1.5 metres (5 ft) blanket of peat was excavated away from the stones in the mid 1800s thus creating endless theories, some reasonable, some a tad ridiculous. Theories.... where the hell would we be without them? The slender stones embedded into the ground are Lewisian gneiss, which geological experts believe to be amongst the oldest rock types anywhere in the world, similar in age to Mick Jagger and his affiliated ancient Stones. It is most evident, however, that Callanish is ageing considerably better and is clearly in far superior condition, although like the other Stones tone deaf.

Callanish is not an isolated enigma and, although by far the largest site, it is just one of almost twenty megalithic monuments in relatively close proximity on the Isle of Lewis, and thus it would appear to have been some form of regional centre in prehistoric times. It is quite probable that these stone circles were used as meeting points by our ancestors for religious purposes, astronomical observances and basic trading of goods where Marks & Spencer may well have considered the potential benefits of a smallish store with takeaway avocado and prawn sandwiches. It has been observed that when looking south along one of the stone avenues the midsummer full moon sets perfectly behind Clisham, the highest mountain in the Western Isles.

The age of Callanish as mentioned rules out any Christian involvement, and one local legend claims that the stones were once giants who lived on the island but were turned to stone by Saint Kieran when they refused to be Christianised. Arguably not the best method of conversion to Christianity and the teachings of our Lord but he can hold a grudge. Latterly it has even been seriously suggested that the stones were erected by Martians arriving from outer space in a flying saucer, but considering the stringent building control and planning permission restrictions enforced by the Western Isles Council, this is highly unlikely. The most frequently asked questions concerning Callanish relate to the methods of transportation and erection of these massive stones. None of the locals can remember any such activity in the area, and as the Lewis based civil engineering firm of J.A.Mackenzie Ltd would not be established for another 4,950 years or so it is a sure bet they were not invited to quote for the contract.

Whilst the true origin and purpose of the Callanish Stones will never be known, they proudly stand as a monument to the ingenuity, abilities and culture of the most ancient of Scots.

Items available at Callanish Visitor Centre, Isle of Lewis.

Dec 2000

The Night Watch

CARLOWAY BROCH

On the extreme north western edge of the British Isles and with naught but some 3,000 miles of the Atlantic Ocean to the old colony of North America, stands one of the few remaining brochs in existence, the name given to a unique type of Iron Age fort. Not far from the wild waves and unpredictable moods of the Atlantic, Dun Carloway on the Isle of Lewis was built over 2,000 years ago, thus making it one of the oldest existing fortifications in Britain. In typical broch fashion it is a conical stone tower some 9 metres (30 ft) high with outer and inner parallel stone walls, using stone slab stairs which cleverly tie together these two walls, whilst this stairway spirals it's way up to the top of the structure for access to the different levels. There would likely have been 4 timber floored levels within for living accommodation, and entry is still solely by a very low doorway thus ensuring any unwanted visitors could be suitably dealt with, clobbered over the head, decapitated or the like, as any the intruder had to enter in a crouching position. The stonework is truly incredible and one has to marvel at such masonry skills more than 2,000 years ago.

It was last fully occupied circa 1300, which is quite incredible for a structure which can claim to have been lived in continuously for about 1,300 years, and even since then it has not been without periodic occupants. In 1500s there is an account of the continuous clan feud between the MacAulays and the dominant Morrisons on the Isle of Lewis, whereby following a cattle raid by a group of Morrisons, one Donald Cam MacAulay climbed the outer wall using the blade of his dirk (knife) between the stone layers and on reaching the top, he threw burning heather down into the broch thus smothering to death the party of Morrisons trapped inside, the other MacAulays having blocked the doorway to prevent any of them escaping. The broch was even being used by a family as a dwelling in 1870s, albeit presumably without en-suite bathroom, or 5G broadband, or even roof.

April 2013   Dun Càrlabhagh

GEARRANNAN BLACKHOUSE VILLAGE

Less than a century ago there would be hundreds of small villages like Gearrannan (also known as Garenin) all over the Highlands and Islands of Scotland but excluding ruinous sites none now remain other than this totally rebuilt village, the laborious work carried out by skilled craftsmen, thatch roofers, and stone masons. No rusting Ford Transits poorly signed with 'free estimates' (who ever paid £100 to be told their new kitchen would cost £5,000?) were seen on site. Much of the renovation was carried out in 2000 and this small coastal village in Carloway on the Isle of Lewis now consists of a fine restaurant, gift shop, working museum complete with Harris Tweed loom, exhibition, auditorium and four self contained croft houses to accommodate from two persons to a bunkhouse for up to sixteen folk with each house named after the last family who lived there, this being as recent as the early 1970s. All the houses have been superbly fitted out in beautiful styles with many modern conveniences. Gearrannan is a truly unique and excellent place to stay situated on the edge of a small bay with amazing views out over the Atlantic and dramatic cliff top walks.

Whilst not at Gearrannan but not that many miles away and still on Lewis, the mother of the disgraced former President Trump, Mary Anne MacLeod was born in 1912 in Tong, three miles from Stornoway in a humble croft house before in 1930 she emigrated to New York looking for work as a domestic servant and in fact she did rather well for herself 6 years after her arrival in the old colony by marrying property developer Frederick Trump, being the founder of the Trump property business. In June 2008 their son flew into Stornoway to visit his mother's birth place and clearly when he saw his roots he shamefully spent less than a minute inside the house showing no interest whatsoever in the house or his hosts' chat on island life in his mother's days. Clearly he felt much more at home that night in his luxurious Turnberry Hotel and it must be said that the islanders views of this man who would unfortunately later became the most powerful in the world need not be printed here. After Trump's appalling comments and criminal actions following his election loss in late 2020, the 'island' stated that Lewis disowns this vulgar bully and 'let this be an end to our disgrace' albeit of course it is not their disgrace but his. The islanders clearly not alone regarding the man CNN News referred to as a 'lying sack of depravity'.

To conclude, for an enjoyable Lewis croft house experience, Gearrannan certainly has the edge over Tong.

Aug 2001   Croft House

March 2001

The High Street

IMPRESSIONS OF LEWIS

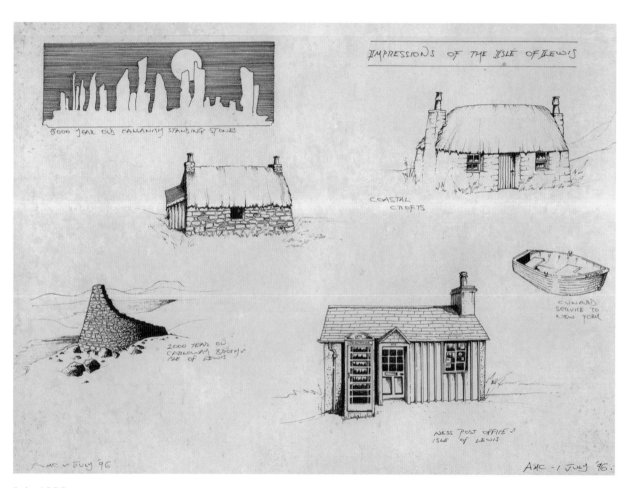

IMPRESSIONS OF THE ISLE OF LEWIS

5000 YEAR OLD CALLANISH STANDING STONES

COASTAL CROFTS

2000 YEAR OLD CARLOWAY BROCH, ISLE OF LEWIS

CUNARD SERVICE TO NEW YORK

NESS POST OFFICE, ISLE OF LEWIS

July 1996

IMPRESSIONS OF HARRIS

IMPRESSIONS OF THE ISLE OF HARRIS

THE HARRIS TWEED AUTHORITY
- Ughdarras a Chlo Hearaich -

RODEL CHURCH,
BUILT IN 1520s
BY ALASDAIR CROTACH

ARDVOURLIE CASTLE
ON LOCH SEAFORTH

THE HARRIS TWEED GANG.

HOUSES AT
FHOINNSBHAIGH

CLACH MHICLEOID
STANDING STONE

RING OF BRIGHT WATER

AMC - 9 JULY '96.

July 1996

63

LOCH SEAFORTH

When crossing from the Isle of Lewis to the Isle of Harris, both 'Isles' in fact sharing the same island mass despite the understandable confusion that they are separate (which they ain't) one will pass by steep rocky hillsides leading to mountains on one side and an incredible far distanced view out over Loch Seaforth on the other side. Until a few years ago the actual border if you can call it that was at a tiny stone bridge on a single track road with hardly noticeable signs on either side informing the traveller that they had now passed into another territory and whilst there is no conflict these days, centuries ago straying over this border could result in clan warfare between the Morrisons of Lewis and the MacLeods of Harris with much blood spilt and not a few cattle (and virgins) missing. Whilst the abducted virgins still remains a present day issue, beef products are generally now sourced at Tesco and Co-op in Stornoway.

March 2001   Loch Seaforth

March 2001   Gearrannan Midnight

MINDSCAPES

Jan 2001   Boat to No-where

Feb 2001   Coastal Croft

Feb 2000   Harris Beach

Feb 2000   Land of Grey & Pink

Isolation

Feb 2000 Wee Tigs Beach

SCOTTISH HISTORY

including exclusive images for

NATIONAL TRUST FOR SCOTLAND

BATTLE OF BANNOCKBURN

The Anxious Garrison

The besieged Stirling Castle was actually the root cause of the Battle of Bannockburn in 1314. Sir Edward Bruce the hot headed brother of Robert Bruce, King of Scots had recklessly agreed with the English governor Sir Philip Moubray that if Stirling Castle was not relieved by the English by 24 June, the castle would be surrendered to the Scots. The King was livid with his brother for making such an agreement as he was ill prepared to oppose the might of England, whilst the English King, Edward II, felt that to save face with his own rebellious and powerful lords and nobles he had no option but to relieve Stirling and thus headed north with an army of over 20,000. The Bruce with a much lesser army of 7,500, skillfully used the natural features of the land and combined with brilliant military tactics defeated the might of English chivalry whereby Edward II fled back over the border with the remnants of his army. The castle duly surrendered.

Lesser known is the origination of the Scottish saltire, this resulting from another Scots (albeit Picts) victory at Athelstaneford in East Lothian almost 500 years earlier in AD 832 when on the day of the battle against invading Angles from the North of England, the clouds formed a cross over the blue sky and the Scots took this as a sign of a supportive Saint Andrew and (with him rooting for them) won the day.

Exclusive for National Trust for Scotland. Available at Bannockburn visitor centre.

NATIONAL TRUST *for* **SCOTLAND**

The Anxious Garrison

BATTLE OF BANNOCKBURN

The War Sword

A variety of weapons were used at the Battle of Bannockburn on that June day in 1314 including spears, lances, long bows, maces, daggers, battle axes (the latter which Robert the Bruce, King of Scots niftly used at Bannockburn to crack open Sir Henry de Bohun's skull) and of course swords. The most widely used sword during this period by both the Scots & English was the war sword developed for close hand combat. This weapon with a length of over one metre (3 ft) was principally used by highly trained knights & men-at-arms, and could be used either with one hand for stabbing motions or two hands for hacking through enemy lines with much bone crunching.

When the English archers were proving ineffective at the battle having been decimated by Sir Robert Keith's light Scots cavalry, such weaponry became prominent along with Bruce's schiltrons (masses of up to 500 spearmen not unlike a rather large aggressive hedgehog) in pressing the might of the English army backwards on that 24th June in 1314 when the English forces fled or drowned in the Burn of Bannock.

Exclusive for National Trust for Scotland. Available at Bannockburn visitor centre.

NATIONAL TRUST *for* **SCOTLAND**

Aug 2019

The War Sword

BATTLE OF KILLIECRANKIE

Whilst being a notable natural feature of a tree lined gorge straddling the fast flowing River Garry in Perthshire, a major battle took place here at Killiecrankie on 27th July 1689 this being the first engaged battle between the Jacobites and Government forces 57 years before the final outcome at Culloden. The lawful King of Britain, the Catholic James VII of Scots and James II of England had been deposed and exiled to France, with the throne being taken over by the Dutch Protestant William of Orange in January 1689.

The few remaining troops in Scotland loyal to James (hence the name Jacobites derived from Jacobus, Latin for James) were led by John Graham, Viscount Claverhouse affectionately known as Bonnie Dundee who promptly embarked on raising an army of Scots to fight for James' cause culminating in some 3,000 Highlanders although this soon depleted with some 500 deserters. Scottish government troops of over 4,000 were raised and led by General Hugh MacKay (also a Scot) to annihilate the Viscount and his army before Jacobite supporting troops arrived from Ireland. The Scottish redcoat army was strung out along the north bank of the river when MacKay became aware the Jacobite army was heading south to meet them. Both armies faced each other for a couple of hours before Bonnie Dundee ordered the attack against the thinly spread out redcoats of lines only three deep which indeed dispensed with some 600 Highlanders being cut down with musket fire. Quickly the advantage of the single shot musket was lost as the Highlanders crashed through with claymore, axe and dirk. The redcoats became disorganised and the battle concluded with Bonnie Dundee leading a cavalry charge through the enemy. The government army had lost some 2,000 men and the Jacobites around 800. Tragically Bonnie Dundee was killed by a stray musket shot to the head after the battle was won and whilst it was a resounding victory for the Jacobite cause, they had lost their best military commander. It must be remembered that Culloden and Killiecrankie were not battles between the Scots and the English as often thought.

What should be seen if visited is the famous Soldier's Leap rocky precipice where one fleeing redcoat Donald MacBean jumped 5.5 metres (18 ft) over the River Garry to escape his Jacobite pursuers. Much of the area is a National Trust for Scotland site with visitor centre, river walkways, and much wildlife to be spotted as well of course as the Soldier's Leap, but don't try to jump it.

It is claimed that the last wolf in Great Britain was shot near Killiecrankie in 1680. There is ongoing debate on the reintroduction of wolves into Scotland's Highlands but at present if you want to see these magnificent animals you'll have to visit the Highland Wildlife Park near Aviemore.

Aug 2019   The Soldier's Leap

Grey Wolves

Sept 2019

Pass of Killiecrankie

GLENCOE MASSACRE

On 13 February 1692 the infamous massacre of 38 MacDonald clansfolk took place in Glencoe carried out ruthlessly by 120 Government Campbell redcoats, fellow Scots from neighbouring Argyll. Amongst the dead was the Clan Chief, Alasdair McIan, and with their livestock being slaughtered and their homesteads being burnt out, the surviving MacDonalds fled into the cold winter mountains to escape the muskets and bayonets of these same Campbells who had shared their MacDonald hospitality, food and lodgings for over a week, before the order was issued to commence the extermination of what was regarded as a rogue clan by the British Government, intent on eliminating Jacobite support.

More MacDonalds perished in the freezing conditions under the shadows of The Three Sisters, being those haunting mountains overlooking the place of this treacherous massacre of the MacDonalds of Glencoe by the Campbells of Argyll on British Government orders.

The monument in nearby Ballachulish was erected in 1883 by a MacDonald descendant of the slain Chief, Alasdair McIan.

Exclusive for National Trust for Scotland. Available at Glencoe visitor centre.

The Three Sisters and Memorial

June 2019   The Ruins of Glencoe

GLENFINNAN MONUMENT

Arrival At Glenfinnan...the Start of the '45

The welcome of Charles Edward Stuart (Bonnie Prince Charlie) and his handful of followers on the shores of Loch Shiel on 19 August 1745 was a somewhat muted event with many of the Highland clan chiefs totally ignoring his summons to rally and others a tad reluctant to partake in another Jacobite rebellion.

Cameron of Lochiel, who the next year would loose many clansmen fighting for the prince at the Battle of Culloden in 1746, commented on the prince's arrival with *"whoever advised him to undertake it, has a great deal to answer for"*, whilst many other clan chiefs had advised the prince to go back home to France. As it turned out the prince had not been at all honest with these chiefs about the military support he claimed that he had secured, as soon became apparent.

Exclusive for National Trust for Scotland. Available at Glenfinnan visitor centre.

NATIONAL TRUST *for* **SCOTLAND**

July 2019

July 2019

Monument to a Fool

BATTLE OF CULLODEN

Blood Skies Over Culloden

On 16 April 1746, the depleted, tired, weary (after a fruitless night march to surprise attack the enemy), and hungry Jacobite army of some 5,500 Highlanders faced the fresh Government army of 7,500 redcoats on a misty morning at Culloden five miles east of Inverness.

Leanach Cottage was located within the redcoat lines and close to the only area of serious redcoat losses during the battle when the Highlanders charged through the redcoat's left flank, but regardless, the battle was over within an hour. 1,250 Jacobites lay dead with a similar number wounded whilst only 50 redcoats were killed. The bloodshed continued under the orders of the Duke of Cumberland, (King George II's son) aptly nicknamed The Butcher who instructed that all the wounded and escaping survivors must be shot or bayoneted to death. No prisoners were taken or quarter given.

Bonnie Prince Charlie's experienced general, Lord George Murray had advised a strategic retreat whilst waiting on further clan reinforcements to arrive and commented "I do not like the ground, it is certainly not proper for Highlanders" but unfortunately and as was his habit, the prince would not listen to sound military advice, and so the last full scale battle on British soil culminated in a brutal slaughter of Highlanders by the Government's redcoat army on Culloden's blood soaked Drummossie Moor.

The prince escaped back to France and lived the rest of his life in drunken luxury whilst his Jacobite followers and many innocent folk were hunted down, executed and persecuted for years after.

Exclusive for National Trust for Scotland. Available at Culloden visitor centre.

June 2019

Blood Skies Over Culloden

HADRIAN'S WALL

Keeping The Caledonians Out

As some skool children (unlike their parents) know as indeed any remaining Romans, Hadrian's Wall is not and never has been on the border with today's Scotland but is totally in England varying from half a mile from the border on the west and 68 miles over on the east but nevertheless this incredible construction by the Romans was built to keep those pesky pre-Scots the Romans called Caledonians at bay and to prevent their savage barbarity spilling over into Roman occupied Britannia, thus whilst not actually in Scotland this has sneaked into the book as a Scottish-related-albeit-not-in-Scotland-bit.

So named after the Emperor Hadrian this amazing feat of Roman technique, knowledge and ability commenced building in AD 122 and indeed what a construction project this 73 mile project was. Spaced every Roman mile was a two turreted small castle manned by a static garrison of around 24 legionnaires and every 5 miles a substantial fort with quick response troops of infantry and cavalry. These damn Caledonians were clearly a bloody nuisance. Mind you, the Callies were a wily lot and it is suspected that rather than climbing over the wall they sneaked round the two ends when the legionnaires were having their supper at tea time. With so much involved in building a wall 2.5 metres (8 ft) wide x 73 miles, with some 80 mile-castles and major forts along the way it is quite incredible to think that the Wall was completed by the 3 occupying legions in 6 years using not a single slave but Roman legionnaire masons supported by numerous auxiliary soldiers, thus somewhat quicker than the disastrous Edinburgh Trams project. The incompetent buffoons in Edinburgh City Council could well have learnt quite a bit about project management from the Romans.

The route of the Wall can be followed close to a national path most surprisingly called the Hadrian's Wall Path whilst there are car parks at the 'best' bits (Chesters Roman Fort, Housesteads Fort, & Vindolanda or Vindaloo or something) for those who don't fancy trekking 73 bloody miles, so thus just about everyone. It is estimated that some 90% of the original Wall has disappeared as over the centuries many local folk looked upon the Wall more as Hadrian's Builders Merchants Ltd which stocked perfectly cut blocks "just the right size" for my castle, farmhouse, cottage, sheep pen or Holiday Inn Express with the added benefit that all the material was free excluding delivery and VAT (Vindolanda Added Tax).

1971. Early AMC (aged 14) depictions of battles between Romans and Caledonians

Feb 2021   The Wall

KILMARTIN GLEN

Guardians of Ballymeanoch

This area of Argyll a few miles north of Lochgilphead has an abundance of ancient Scottish history including standing stones, stone circles, burial cairns, henges, and ancient rock carvings going back over 6,000 years. Indeed it has the most comprehensive concentration of Neolithic and Bronze Age remains on the Scottish mainland with 800 ancient monuments within a 6 mile radius. There is also an Iron Age hill fort at Dunadd being an excellent defensive position on a rocky crag. This was the centre of power for the ancient (pre-Scotland) kingdom of Dalriada (Dal Riata) and seat of the Dalriadan kings, this being after the Romans left Britain circa AD 410 as they had a bit of a problem on the home front with Visigoths (ancient German thugs but lots of them) attacking Rome. There are chronicled records of a siege of Dunadd in AD 683, the outcome, however, not recorded. In AD 736, Oengus (these days Angus), King of the Picts conquered Dalriada, and extended this into his own territory of Pictavia, so as can be seen the ancient Scots were frequently at each other's throats so a bit like now really. In fact around this period of history today's Scotland was made up of some 7 separate conflicting kingdoms.

One neolithic site at Ballymeanoch consists of a row of stones going back more than 4,000 years, the tallest being 4 metres (13 ft) whilst the two middle stones are heavily carved with prehistoric art ring and cup marks and in addition there are also a stone circle, henge earthwork feature and burial cairn here.

In the village of Kilmartin in the old manse there is an excellent informative historical museum with cafe and historical book & gift shop conveniently opposite a splendid pub in the Kilmartin Hotel for the weary traveller who desires a more substantial drink than coffee.

These paintings were done on the request of the Kilmartin Museum in 2019 and are exclusively supplied on certain products for the museum shop.

June 2019

Sentinels at Kilmartin

PEEL OF LUMPHANAN

Death Of MacBeth

Shakespeare's tragically inaccurate portrayal of MacBeth is far more tragic than the tragedy itself and in modern times Bill the Bard would be facing serious legal action for defamation, slander and indeed accused of 'fake news'.

In reality and historically MacBeth was one of Scotland's most capable honourable kings, and his wife called Gruoch who rather than a horrendous manipulative evil bitch was extremely religious and through her royal connections helped Macbeth on his path to the throne. That year was 1040 and indeed whilst MacBeth did kill the war mongering and incompetent King Duncan I, he was not stabbed whilst he slept but killed on the battlefield by MacBeth defending his Moray lands as at that time MacBeth was Earl of Moray and Duncan rather had it in for him. MacBeth became King of Scots a few weeks after Duncan's death and throughout his 17 year reign he ruled with a fair hand and Scotland became prosperous with both himself and Gruoch spreading the word of Christianity. He only brought men to arms to subdue unjustified rebellion whilst he introduced some of Scotland's earliest laws including officers of the court defending women and orphans anywhere in his realm and also albeit with much opposition daughters having the same rights as sons as to inheritance. In 1050 he and Gruoch travelled to Rome to meet the Pope for a papal jubilee whilst they donated much to the poor en-route. Hardly the villain portrayed by W.S. Esq when in truth other characters in the play are the true villains.

MacBeth's cousin and the bastard (a real one) son of Duncan I, Malcolm (known as Big Head as he had an abnormally large bonce) hated his popular cousin and sought the throne for himself gaining support from England and in particular the Earl Siward of Northumbria. Malcolm Big Head over the next few years sought any allies he could to bring about trouble and battle with the king which culminated in the Battle of Lumphanan, some 25 miles west of Aberdeen. In fact it was more a skirmish as MacBeth had been defeated by Malcolm some days before and was retreating back to the safety of his Moray earldom with his depleted surviving force. On 15 August 1057 Malcolm caught up with this small force and annihilated them reputedly leaving MacBeth to last and where it is said he was beheaded on the spot close to where the Peel of Lumphanan, a 13th century earthwork castle was later built although some claim the site of the fort is actually where the king was decapitated. There is a stone close by called MacBeth's Stone some say the one on which he was beheaded, albeit his final resting place was on the holy isle of Iona, the residence of numerous previous deceased Scottish monarchs, some good, some not so.

Upon MacBeth's death, Gruoch's gentle but not exactly monarch material son Lulach (MacBeth's stepson) was crowned king but Malcolm getting somewhat impatient for the throne had Lulach treacherously murdered after only 7 months and took the crown for himself. Like his father Duncan, Malcolm III proved to be a totally useless albeit constantly war-faring king with little historically to his credit so it was no real disappointment when in 1093 he fell into an English trap in Northumbria where he was tricked away from the Scottish army under an English flag of truce and felled by sword with his skull split open by his deceiving escort.

Thus tragically MacBeth, a great king was respectively both superseded and ultimately followed by war mongering father and son brutes with their only interest being in ruthless power and seldom the well being of the realm. Neither monarch historically contributed a single benefit to Scotland. Equally tragic is the defamatory garbage one Bill Shakespeare wrote about a truly great man and king, and his kindly wife.

Feb 2021 (Ghosts in sky, July 1973 English O-Level exam. FAIL, drawing apparently not allowed)

June 2019

Gateway to Kilmartin Glen

'OUTLANDER' LOCATIONS

from the TV series

CALLANISH STANDING STONES

Used universally for decades in all types of films and TV series and even pictured on an Ultravox album cover, the Callanish Stones indeed convey a striking image particularly with that high dominant central stone, so when the writers and producers of 'Outlander' set about the ideal location to pop back in time, ancient standing stones clearly seemed like a good idea, albeit that the real ones are far, far away from the story line being way up on the Isle of Lewis.

There is much more detail about these Stones, these being older than that southern Stonehenge, earlier in this book, so there is little more to mention here other than whilst in reality there are no trees surrounding the Callanish Stones, a few birches nevertheless suit a perfect starting point for those time travellers on TV.

The visitor centre at Callanish is well worth visiting with an excellent local produce cafe, gift shop and auditorium/exhibition room whilst the panoramic views in all directions from the Stones themselves are quite breath-taking.

Dec 2000   The Mists of Time

Items available at Callanish Visitor Centre, Isle of Lewis.

Dec 2000

Piper at the Gates of Dawn

BATTLE OF CULLODEN

The Last Dusk Afore Battle

The principal character in Outlander, Jamie Fraser, is loosely based on the actual accounts of a Jacobite called Fraser who fought at the ill fated Battle of Culloden and survived a mass execution of his fellow Highlanders, so the author Diana Gabaldon thus developed this character. Despite all the fantasy and fiction in the TV series the portrayal of the battle and aftermath in the series is relatively accurate.

Against much intelligent advice from his closest advisers and with unknown support in Scotland, Charles Edward Stuart (Bonnie Prince Charlie) had in July 1745 secretly arrived from France with a handful of followers in the Outer Hebrides, but he was totally lacking troops, arms and funds, and yet he still proceeded with the '45 Rising' at Glenfinnan in the name of the Stuart claim for the British throne. On his arrival a few Highland clans loyal to the Jacobite cause offered support but most did not. With some reluctance an army did, however, muster increasing in size as it proceeded south. Initially the foray went very well and Perth and Edinburgh fell without major resistance. The Prince, however, far too quickly decided on a dramatic invasion of England right down to London where he wrongly believed numerous English lords supported the Jacobite cause, and against the advice of his war council, the most notable being his General Lord George Murray, the army proceeded on the venture into England. By winning battles and by-passing government divisions of redcoats, whilst under the leadership of Murray they made it as far south as Derby only 125 miles from a panic stricken London convinced that a Highland army would soon take possession of the capital. If that had happened indeed British history could have changed dramatically. However, it was not to be. Support in England was discovered as minimal and the army was far south and very exposed to attack from the rear. Lord Murray insisted on a withdrawal to Scotland, and the Prince thereafter sulked denied his somewhat unlikely prize of the British Crown. Relations deteriorated between the Prince and his war council and he barely spoke to them on the return journey. Eventually on 16 April 1746 he got his way to make a stand against the government army at Culloden just east of Inverness, but again this was much against the advice of his betters.

Following an ill advised and aborted attempted night raid on the government forces, a tired, starving and demoralised Highlander army of 5,500 returned and took up position on a boggy moor against a fresh much better equipped military army of 7,500 redcoat soldiers. The battle started with ineffective artillery fire from the Jacobites followed by effective artillery fire from the government troops which tore through the Highlander ranks, this followed by grapeshot from the government cannons which caused much more devastation. The Jacobites in frustration and anger bravely charged against the government army lines where redcoat musket fire felled hundreds more and then followed hand to hand combat with some Highlanders breaking through. Within an hour, however, the battle was over with some 1,250 Jacobites dead and yet only 50 redcoat fatalities. The slaughter continued well after with the rout and the 'Butcher', Duke of Cumberland (King George II's son) commanded that all fleeing and wounded Jacobites be bayoneted to death on the spot and some 1,000 more Jacobites were killed by such cold brutality after the battle was over. One cavalry officer recounted "Our light horse and dragoons were sent after them, and strew'd the road for 5 miles with dead bodies". Leanach Cottage which still stands to this day was in the middle of the redcoat lines, its occupants having wisely fled beforehand.

The last pitched battle fought on British soil is often mistakenly regarded as a battle between the Scots and the English but this is not the case. This was the eventual final outcome between the Jacobites supporting the Stuarts as the rightful monarchs of Britain and the Hanoverians under King George II. In fact amongst the government troops were Scottish redcoat regiments including 360 Scots Fusiliers infantry and 200

Argyleshire infantry, being Campbells under John Campbell, 5th Duke of Argyll. Taking into account the local redcoat militia tragically Highland brother fought against brother and father against son.

The blame for the disastrous defeat lies totally with the incompetent Prince Charles Edward Stuart whose many failings included refusing to wait for Jacobite reinforcements from Inverness, chose the boggy Drumossie Moor as the battle ground against sound military advice, and didn't want to abandon the previous night's futile raid further tiring the exhausted Highlander army. Despite the romantic and heroic perception of this charming prince depicted in an extremely dreadful 1948 film starring David Niven (whilst the prince was hiding from the redcoats, Niven was hiding from the critics and reviews), and latterly on Walkers shortbread tins, Charlie (a right one) was in truth an impulsive fool, who through arrogance, lying about guaranteed military support from France and England, and ignoring the advice of his war council, totally failed and finished forever the Jacobite cause. He deserted his army whilst the loyal clans and commanders were determined to fight on, and then fled to France in cowardly disgrace, where he contented himself with whores and booze for the rest of his drunken life, whilst his loyal Jacobites in Scotland still eager to fight for his cause were being persecuted, tortured, slaughtered and demeaned for years by the Hanoverian government and their redcoats. The real tragic conclusion of the Jacobite cause is that so many thousands died in vain for this Bonnie Prince Charlie. Many things he was but hero he was not. He is best remembered printed on shortbread tins, a most fitting tribute for a biscuit. What is without doubt is in truth he remains one of Scotland's most disgraced figures.

June 2019   The Last Dusk Afore Battle

DOUNE CASTLE (CASTLE LEOCH)

Built in the 14th century, on the foundations of an ancient Roman fort, on a fork of land where the River Teith and Ardoch Burn meet, Doune Castle was always well protected by these natural moats. The castle was built by Robert Stewart, the Earl of Fife, and later Duke of Albany, a great grandson of Robert the Bruce, and brother to King Robert III. However the Duke was an unscrupulous, ambitious and highly treacherous man, who controlled most of Scotland, whilst his scholarly but feeble brother sat on the throne, or for most of the time did not. Their notorious brother was Alexander, Earl of Buchan, known as "The Wolf of Badenoch", who controlled North East Scotland as his own Kingdom, and who had a reputation for hunting down men as sport, when he bored with wild boar, wolves, deer and the like. A huge, strong and most brutal man was also responsible for burning down Elgin Cathedral in 1390, with his army of "wyld wykkyd helandmen" to prove his total disrespect for his brothers and the Church (see Lochindorb Castle). Another brother was Walter Stewart, Lord of Brechin, a drunken sod who all of his life never sobered up long enough to be worthy of comment. These 4 great grandsons of the Bruce were clearly all so different from each other but sadly there was not one that he could ever have been proud of. Robert III in truth had no desire to be King but was obliged to the title being the eldest son of Robert II. His name was actually John, but in light of the disastrous reigns of John Balliol, puppet king of Edward I, and the appalling King John of England, who was detested by all his barons, John was regarded as a lousy name for a monarch, so Robert suggested he also used the name Robert. Thus there now was Robert III the King, and his devious brother Robert the Regent. After the King titled his son David Stewart, as Duke of Rothesay, being the first duke in Scotland, the Regent determined not to be outdone, self styled himself the Duke of Albany, the ancient Pictish name for all of Scotland, clearly going one better.

Albany built Doune Castle some 8 miles from Stirling Castle, that being the seat of the King, where he could not only keep an eye on his weak brother, but also any lords and visitors who came from other parts of the kingdom, and his network of spies left little undisclosed. It is quite likely that Albany had James, 2nd Earl of Douglas (see Tantallon Castle) murdered by the Earl's own armour bearer during the Battle of Otterburn in 1388 where the Scottish army led by the Douglas soundly defeated an opposing English army on their own soil in Northumberland, led by "Hotspur', or more officially Sir Henry Percy, son and heir to the Earl of Northumberland. Douglas was the most powerful family in Scotland and within days, could raise tens of thousands of armed men, whereas the Stewarts, even as the Royal Family, could barely raise two thousand of their own. Such were the Kings of Scots so highly dependant on military support from their earls and lords. The Douglas could always pose a threat to the Stewarts and clearly Robert Stewart had felt their power must be contained.

The Douglas successor to the earldom, Sir Archibald the Grim, 3rd Earl of Douglas was closer to the Duke of Albany and posed less of a threat, although it soon became apparent to Albany that the Douglases still largely did as suited them. Years later Albany planned the abduction and murder by slow starvation of his brother's son, the heir to the throne, the young and handsome David, Duke of Rothesay, who was a much stronger character than his pitiful father the King, and clearly loathed Albany making no secret to his ambition to become King and sack his devious uncle as Regent. Neither of these murders, along with others, could ever be proven to be on Albany's instructions as he had a bad but clever habit of having his chosen murderers likewise murdered to silence them forever. Albany, cold and ruthless, was intensely hated, but much feared and few nobles, other than the Douglases ever saw any advantage in crossing him. With good cause, he clearly trusted no-one, and even though Doune Castle was a substantial and well defended fortress, his own tower and accommodation could be internally secured and isolated against any attack from within, in such event that even his own garrison turned against him.

Albany's legacy hardly helped his son, Murdoch Stewart, the next Lord of Doune and Regent of Scotland, who was executed in 1425, by King James I, David's younger brother who had never forgiven his uncle Robert for the foul murder by starvation in a damp prison cell, of the older brother he idolised, and who should have been the rightful King of Scots. It is said that the fingers of David's hands were gnawed to the bones as in his desperation he chewed them beyond recognition. Albany died, as Regent of Scotland, a peaceful death aged over 80 in 1420, many clearly having hoped for an otherwise closure, and it must have infuriated the new King James, that Albany had cheated him out of an excruciatingly nasty death. Having Murdoch executed was likely scant consolation. James I had much loathing for the Albany line of the family after his 18 years as a captive of King Henry IV in London, not being released until 1424, with Albany having done bugger all to attempt his freedom either by invasion or negotiation, clearly having decided that his nephew as monarch in his patch was undesirable.

Centuries later, in 1745/46 the castle was captured by the Jacobite forces in support of Bonnie Prince Charlie, and was used as a prison, although one prisoner did escape with the classic use of descending a rope of knotted cloth from a window. Such happened in history, not just Hollywood.

The castle, to this day, remains extremely impressive with the main tower almost 35 metres (115 ft) high, and most of the walling 3 metres (10 ft) thick. The huge kitchens and sizeable banquet halls show that despite the devious nature of the Duke of Albany; as a shrewd politician, he was not averse to holding huge banquets to attempt to manipulate Scotland's nobility only a few miles from the Royal seat of power, although in reality Scotland was governed from Doune, not Stirling. Most recently, however, Doune features prominently as Castle Leoch in Outlander.

Jan 1999

MIDHOPE CASTLE (LALLYBROCH)

Somewhat better known to Outlander fans as Lallybroch, the laird's home of Jamie Fraser, Midhope Castle is only a few miles west of the Forth Bridges although well hidden in the Hopetoun Estate. Since the TV series this castle has over recent years become quite a visitor attraction which was eluded by any such historical events.

Unlike Doune Castle, Midhope does not have much history of any significant interest being the typical tower house design built in the 16th century with five floors and a later added lower wing. It originally belonged to the Drummonds then passed to the Livingston Earls of Linlithgow before the Hopes took ownership and who used the castle to house farm workers when the expansive luxurious palace of Hopetoun House was being built. It thereafter fell into disrepair and is derelict with only the exterior being used for Outlander.

Whilst Midhope can be visited for a fee payable to some bloke in a tiny wooden hut at a gate (closed most of the time), you won't get much for your buck other than a few photos of the outside but still a must for serious fans if they can find the place.

Jan 2020

Dec 2000   Callanish - Rock Solid

ISLE OF SKYE

See also Talisker Distillery, Dunvegan Castle and Duntulm Castle

THE OLD MAN OF STORR

Some 6 miles north of Portree on the Isle of Skye although well visible for many miles south of that small town, The Old Man of Storr proudly protrudes against the varying skies backdrop. This 50 metres (164 ft) high basalt rock pinnacle is part of the Trotternish ridge which was formed by a massive landslide and is largely composed of ancient lava flows. Some may recognize it in the opening scenes of one of Ridley Scott's Alien series films 'Prometheus' whilst it also appears in the disturbing yet classic film 'The Wicker Man'. Due to the shape of the pinnacle it has only successfully been climbed a very few times. Many have tried and many have failed.

There are two legends of The Old Man of Storr, one being that part of the range is an old man's face, and the other that Trotternish was the burial ground of a massively huge giant and the pinnacle is his thumb protruding through from his grave. There does not seem to be much historical evidence for either.

Storr is Norse for 'Great Man' which would have originated from the centuries of brutal raids on the Scottish islands by the Norse Vikings and the times when parts of north-west Scotland were under the control of the Kings of Norway.

Dec 2020   Blue Horizons

Dec 2020

The Cold Man Of Storr

Nov 2020   Guardian of Trotternish

Dec 2020   Lucifer meets Storr

ELGOL

Of course with a great many places the road you are on can suddenly run out and on the Isle of Skye, Elgol is one such place being at the end of the Strathaird peninsula on the rocky shores of Loch Slapin and from those shores over the sea lie the majestic Cuillin Hills of Skye. For a highly recommended and relaxing stay there are two well equipped holiday homes for rent at Strathaird House but anyone hoping for an Indian restaurant within walking distance will be slightly disappointed.

Dec 2020   Midnight from Elgol

Feb 2000   Skye Coastal Croft

MYSTERY

BALLACHULISH GIBBET

The Appin Murder

The murder and subsequent trial which inspired the novel Kidnapped written by Robert Louis Stevenson in 1886, to this day remains an unresolved mystery as to the true identity of the real assassin.

In May 1752 the much hated government factor, one Colin Campbell known as the Red Fox was riding alone on horseback and had set out on his joyful mission of evicting some Stewarts from their homes for non payment of rent when the silence was split by a single musket shot dislodging Campbell from his horse as he plummeted to the ground mortally wounded in the back. It seemed that there was no doubt that the killer was from Clan Stewart and whilst Alan Breck Stewart was suspected but having quickly fled, another Stewart, James of the Glens was quickly arrested.

This murder being 6 years after the Battle of Culloden was assumed to be part of the diehard Jacobite resistance against the Hanoverian monarchy and as the killing took place in Campbell controlled Argyll, the trial against a Stewart, any Stewart was likely to be a farce and indeed it was. The presiding judge was the pro-Hanoverian Archibald Campbell, 3rd Duke of Argyll, 11 of the 15 jurors were Campbells and with the prosecuting lawyer, yup another bloody Campbell. Even though James of the Glens had a concrete alibi and was secretly by the Campbells known not to be the murderer he was nevertheless found guilty and on 8 November 1752 he was hanged proclaiming his innocence and singing Psalm 35 in Gaelic on a specially built gibbet at Ballachulish. Fifteen redcoats were detailed to mount guard at the gibbet to ensure Stewart's decomposing body was not removed for burial and to maintain a warning to all who passed along that high road. It seems clear the Campbells and Hanoverian government were more intent on suppressing further Jacobite sympathies as James of the Glens' corpse was left hanging on the gibbet for 4 years and when the body fell apart beaten by the Scottish weather the bones were held together with wire as warning to deter any anti-Hanoverian perpetrators. Some Campbells later boasted that "anybody could hang a guilty man, but only the head of Clan Campbell hang an innocent one."

It is not known if Alan Breck Stewart was actually the assassin but it later transpired that the murder was planned by 4 other young Stewarts who had previously held a shooting contest between them to determine the best shot and the winner was appointed to kill the Red Fox. It is said that the deed was carried out by young Donald Stewart of Ballachulish and rather than let James hang he wanted to turn himself in but was forcibly restrained by his fellows. What is known is that when the pitiful remains of the corpse were eventually taken down for a permitted by Campbell burial, this Donald washed all the bones before the funeral. However, to add to the mystery some were convinced that the murder was carried out not by a Stewart but a Cameron. After all the Campbells were for long understandably the most despised clan in Scotland. In 1883 the Lord Advocate of Scotland, George Omond in reviewing the old case documents castigated the 3rd Duke of Argyll for consistent bias against James Stewart who in his opinion was clearly sacrificed for political reasons.

Over recent years there has been a petition to pardon James Stewart of the Glens but this was rejected in 2008 as the case being too old to be in the public interest.

Feb 2021

BENNANE CAVE

Cave Of The Cannibals

More often associated with National Geographic and undiscovered tribes living in dense jungles far from civilisation the idea of devouring human flesh does not appeal to the average Scot but one family decided that such would significantly cut down on the weekly shopping bill.

Born in East Lothian in the 16th century Alexander Sawney Bean little fancied following in his father's footsteps as a ditch-digger and together with his partner Black Agnes Douglas, who some thought was a witch, the couple moved through to Ayrshire. What initially started as ambushing, robbing and murdering passers-by the pair soon discovered a taste for their victims. They took over a sea shore cave a few miles from Ballantrae as their residence and over the years the local population dwindled as the Bean family of cannibals grew with 8 sons, 6 daughters, 18 grandsons and 14 granddaughters, none of whom as children ever experienced the delights of Birds Eye fish fingers although indeed fingers did frequently feature at dinner time. Their cave dwelling suited them perfectly as the entrance was cut off by the sea at high tide and they always carried out their horrendous crimes at night and whilst they hid like animals in their cave, certain innocent folk were arrested and hanged for robbery and murder of the missing victims. To throw the authorities off the scent the Beans sometimes discarded human remains on the beach to indicate a wild animal in the location. The local population arranged searches but strangely none ever considered checking out the elongated cave.

Then one night the Beans ambushed a married couple on horseback and whilst the wife was fatally wounded the husband armed with sword and pistol fended off the menacing tribe until by chance a bunch of locals arrived and pursued the Beans (this is where runner beans come from). When word of the atrocities reached the ears of King James IV, he ordered a troop of 400 men with bloodhounds not to rest until these wretches were found and the trail ultimately led to Bennane Cave. On arrival the searchers were horrified and disgusted to find not only the entire deranged dribbling Bean clan but human remains and torsos hanging from the rocky walls, barrels of pickled limbs throughout the cave and heaps of stolen jewellery, clothes and other stuff.

Their execution was unsurprisingly quite brutal after they were all were taken to Edinburgh's Tolbooth Jail in chains. No trial was considered necessary as these non-humans were quite guilty of the foulest of deeds. All the males had their genitals, hands and feet cut off and thus bled to death with Sawney screaming "It isn't over. It will never be over" whilst all the females and kiddibals were burned alive.

Feb 2021

FLANNAN ISLES

The Missing Lighthouse Keepers

It must have seemed one of the most desolate places on Earth, a barren cliff faced and creviced rock outpost constantly beaten by the fury of the Atlantic with the sole building on this tiny remoteness being a lighthouse protecting those at sea whom the inhabitants posted here would never meet and yet this was only 20 miles from the west coast of the Isle of Lewis.

The 23 metres (75 ft) lighthouse built on these Flannan Isles was first lit by paraffin in December 1899 and exactly a year later it became what after more than 120 years remains one of Scotland's unresolved mysteries.

On 15 December 1900 the steamer Archtor from Philadelphia to Leith (Edinburgh) observed that the light was not operating and on arrival reported such to the Northern Lighthouse Board who sent out the lighthouse supply vessel Hesperus from Lewis as soon as weather conditions permitted, this being delayed to 26 December. On arrival it soon became apparent that the 3 lighthouse keepers MacArthur, Marshall and Ducat were nowhere on the island even though the table inside the lighthouse was spread with meat, bread and cheese. The initial thoughts were due to serious stormy weather all three had been washed off the island but there are other theories varying from the ridiculous to the quite possible.

Island folk are renowned for their folklore so initially stories went about that a giant sea bird had carried them away, whereas others thought the 3 keepers had been taken away on a ship of malevolent evil spirits, the Phantom of the Seven Hunters, being vessels lost on the deadly rocks of the Flannans before the lighthouse was built. There was even talk that they had been kidnapped and murdered by foreign agents or villains hiding loot on the island. More plausibly, however, it transpired later that MacArthur was an aggressive man of short temper and in the lonely isolation could well have provoked a fight on the cliff edge ending in disaster, and it was further suggested that one keeper went insane, and killed the other two before throwing himself off the cliffs. It is also suggested that one was washed into the rough sea and the other two drowned trying to save him. It is most probable but by no means certain that Ducat and Marshall were trying to secure equipment during a rough storm and MacArthur who was instructed to remain at the lighthouse went to help them (his oilskin was still on a peg inside), and in the turbulent weather all three were despatched over the cliffs by a massive freak wave. Needless to say, no bodies were ever found.

There are special boat trips to the Flannans and since the lighthouse was automated in 1971 the island has since been totally uninhabited. There is an exhibition and memorial at Breasclete on Lewis where the keeper's families resided when their men were away at the lighthouse, and also where the supply vessel Hesperus was stationed.

Jan 2021

LOCH NESS

Nessie & The Lorry Driver

The first mention of a 'serpent like monster' goes back over 1,450 years to the 6th Century when in AD 570 Saint Columba ordered the beast to be gone after it reputedly attacked one his minions albeit details on this are somewhat vague. Since then there have been many sightings of the creature and over recent decades several dedicated Nessie hunters with boats and incredibly expensive sub water camera equipment and all sorts of technical paraphernalia stuff have been somewhat disappointed that the 90,000 year old prehistoric monster they thought they had eventually discovered actually turned out to be half a dozen Pirellis and Goodyears bobbing about on the murky loch. Nevertheless some people have been adamant they have seen the Loch Ness Monster including a local doctor on call and even a church minister or two. The most famous photograph of the monster showing a small head, twisting neck and upper torso was confirmed as a fake by it's originator some years ago not long before his death disappointing untold thousands of Nessie believers around the world.

One individual claiming continuously to have seen the beast at close quarters was a bloke driving a Scammell lorry working for the civil engineering contractor, A M Carmichael Ltd in 1932 when the firm was constructing 15 miles of new road traversing the loch side. The poor fellow was much ridiculed by his workmates (even though a few others secretly advised they had also seen the creature) but he refused to retract his observation and rather unfairly he was sacked from his job as the site gaffer presumed he had been on the booze and was unfit to drive a lorry in a drunken state, particularly as by then the firm had already lost two steam traction engines which had disappeared over the steep banks into the loch. Interestingly both were recovered by vintage machine enthusiasts in 1980s and fully restored. In those olden days the option of an employment tribunal was not really there so the driver was compelled to find other work. Construction of the new road was frequently held up by cars randomly stopping with the occupants wandering about the construction site desperate to get a glimpse of the monster, even this being in the early 1930s. Nessie, however, lives on in some of the worst films ever made such as 'Beneath Loch Ness' where even the Scots locals have an American drawl, everyone drives a Chevy pickup truck and the hills around the 'loch' are somewhat more Californian than Scottish. Even the local policeman's uniform and accent is California Highway Patrol rather than Police Scotland. Anyone who can even make it half way through that crap, well, must have fallen asleep or died.

Urquhart Castle proudly stands on a rocky promontory jutting out into Loch Ness, near Drumnadrochit (where all sorts of Nessie tat can be bought) and was built circa 1230. The castle has had a most turbulent history with many changes of ownership following battles and sieges not infrequently with the involvement of the powerful and unruly MacDonald 'Lords of the Isles'. The castle's first capture by the English was in 1296 by Edward I, The Hammer of the Scots, although the following year the Scots under Sir Alexander Forbes recaptured it. In 1650 Oliver Cromwell who favoured bombarding castles ignored Urquhart and used a navy frigate to patrol Loch Ness. Lastly garrisoned in 1689 after an unsuccessful attack by Jacobites the castle was largely dismantled by the departing government redcoats in 1691 to prevent the Jacobites using the fortification militarily against them.

The second largest loch in Scotland (the largest being Loch Lomond) at 23 miles (36 km) long, Loch Ness geologically splits the Highlands down a major fault line known as the Great Glen. It's maximum depth is a staggering 227 metres (745 ft) and any activities in looking for a monster have always been hampered by the silty murkiness of those dark cold waters. Interestingly Loch Ness contains more water than all the lakes in England and Wales combined and that's a lot of bloody water.

Nov 2004 (Scammell lorry, March 2000)

DRUMLANRIG CASTLE

The Nicked da Vinci

This relates to the UK's biggest art theft with the thieves mysteriously never caught. In August 2003 two blokes posing as tourists were on a tour of Drumlanrig Castle, north of Dumfries, the ancestral home of the Dukes of Buccleuch, but paying little attention to the blurb from the guide, albeit when they got to a certain place, one put his hand over the young female guide's mouth, whilst the other casually lifted Leonardo da Vinci's painting 'The Madonna of the Yarnwinder' off the wall, whereafter the two climbed out of a window with their booty and made off in a VW Golf. Following this some would say easy theft of a 500 year old masterpiece, reputedly valued at between £30 to £50 million (doesn't seem very precise with a £20 million margin), presumably the local crime prevention officer was called in and on good advice the door locks were changed and the owners advised not to leave the back doors (all of them) open when they went to the shops. Hilariously the investigating police inspector suggested that it was possible that the thieves had visited Drumlanrig previously to case the joint. What? Really? The story does not end there as 4 years later a solicitor from Lancashire and 4 other men were accused of trying to extort £4.25 million from the Duke in return for, and as a reward for locating the painting. It is not clear if that demanded reward included the refund price for the two £6 admission tickets the thieves had purchased for the castle tour. The picture was soon after recovered from a Glasgow solicitor's offices during a police raid in October 2007 and thereafter the 5 men went on trial for a conspiracy plot to extort funds albeit with no charges of theft. After an 8 week trial at Edinburgh's High Court all 5 men walked free still claiming that a reward was due although Buccleuch didn't quite agree. Years later the solicitor sued the Duke for the reward. Drumlanrig Castle is worth a visit but don't expect to see the da Vinci.

Before the theft   After the theft

Since its recovery the painting is on long-term loan from the 10th Duke and is on display in the SCOTTISH NATIONAL GALLERY in Edinburgh, where security is taken a bit more seriously. According to Police Scotland the crime remains an open investigation and they are still seeking the criminals. Well, good luck with that. In this book there is much tragedy, treachery and bloodshed but somehow the theft of a £30 (or could it be £50?) million painting from Scotland's second largest and wealthiest private landowner drew little public sympathy.

AMC 1977

GHOSTS

*See also Borthwick Castle, Dalhousie Castle,
Inveraray Castle, & Lochindorb Castle.*

MELROSE ABBEY

The Melrose Vampire

The Scottish Borders are home to some magnificent albeit ruinous abbeys these being at Jedburgh, Kelso, Dryburgh and Melrose, the latter of Gothic design built from 1136 to 1146 at the request of King David I with extensions being added over a 50 year period and over time this abbey became the final resting place of a few Kings of Scots. This, however, is not what we are looking at here but something most sinister and evil and revealing that Transylvania does not have a monopoly of vampires.

A local chaplain in Melrose like not a few apparently religious Christian priests in both the past and also very much the present tended to find the bad much more enjoyable than the good and this fellow participated in much vice, hunting with packs of dogs, gambling, drinking and whoring and generally was not too interested in those good godly things thus getting him the nickname Hundeprest meaning Dog Priest. When he died in 1196, God wanted bugger all to do with him and considered his soul bad news so the chaplain's soul struggled to find anywhere to call home, and instead his dead ghostly figure roamed the lanes of Melrose attacking and drinking blood from the throats of any folk unwise enough to be out late at night. The local (declining) populace asked the monks from the abbey to rid them of this ghoul which they did; they confronted it, overwhelmed it, did it in (wooden stake and crucifixes not specified) and then burned the corpse letting the winds blow the ashes away. The Hundeprest was not done yet though and returned to the abbey in the form of a bat but could not get inside driven away by the prayers, rantings, ramblings etc of the monks so he descended on the nearby cottage of his former mistress (every chaplain should have one), moaning and screeching at her. The terrified woman ran to the monks for help and the top-monk-in-charge performed an exorcism in her cottage and thereafter four monks took watch at the former chaplain's grave. During the damp cold night the grave opened and the Hundeprest appeared from within understandably scaring the holy crap out of the monks, all except the top-monk-in-charge who laid into the vampire relentlessly beating it with his staff (big stick not the other three monks) shouting prayers and "take that you bastard" at it. This did the trick and the Hundeprest returned to it's grave. The next day the four monks returned and dug up the grave and inside the coffin lay the vampire priest blood still wet on it's lips from an early hours snack victim so it had obviously sneaked out again when the monks had gone to bed. More prayers etc and another bonfire sorted it this time for good as when the ashes blew away over the Lammermuir Hills nothing returned although to this day over 800 years later there are reports of screams coming from the abbey ruins at night and some still claim to see a ghostly figure wandering about in the shadows. Over the centuries there have been other Scots vampires (the elusive Clan MacDrac) who had cast their evil over both Edinburgh and Berwick. There are still some blooding sucking individuals around today, but they tend to work for the banks.

Melrose Abbey also retains a casket containing Robert the Bruce's heart brought back from the Crusades in 1330. The Bruce had always intended to go on the Crusades to the Holy Land and fight the Infidels but never made it as King of Scots turned out to be a full time occupation so on his deathbed in 1329 aged 54 he requested that his heart be taken there by his most loyal friend and brave supporter the 'Good Sir James' (although his son Sir William ultimately proved otherwise, see Hermitage Castle), being the first of what would become the most powerful clan in Scotland, the Douglas. Sir James Douglas was killed in Spain the following year in battle against the Muslim Moors when he threw Bruce's heart at the Infidels shouting "Lead on brave heart, I'll follow thee". The casket was recovered and brought back by Sir William Keith, son of Sir Robert Keith another of the Bruce's noble warrior knights who led a winning Scots cavalry charge at Bannockburn breaking through the English archers.

April 2021

COEFFIN CASTLE, ISLE OF LISMORE

Return to Norway

The slender lush green Isle of Lismore (Gaelic for the Great Garden) in the middle of Loch Linnhe is 10 miles long and 1.5 miles wide and even today less than 200 people live on the island. Much of Scotland's west coast and islands were occupied by the Vikings from the 8th century and Lismore was certainly no exception. Castle Coeffin is named after a Viking prince whose sister Beothail lived in the original castle with some bloke, and following her premature death, she was buried on Lismore. It is said that she haunted the castle in her unhappiness, whether on account of her being dead, or still being on Lismore, where not a lot happens, has never been clarified. A cunning plan was hatched to dig her up, clean them bones, and ship her back to Norway. It worked, and the haunting immediately stopped, so the locals looked on that as a good result and everyone got a better night's sleep. The Vikings were eventually driven out of Lismore by native Islesmen in the early 13th century, not long before King Alexander III cleansed the complete Scottish western seaboard of the dreaded and brutal Norse invaders, following the Battle of Largs in 1263. Lismore had in fact been occupied since ancient times as on the opposite side of the island yet only a mile away is Tirfuir Broch which was built circa 500 BC by the Picts, although very little now remains of this broch and it is much overgrown, unlike other well preserved brochs in the Orkney Islands, Shetland Islands, and the Western Isles (see Carloway Broch).

The newer Coeffin Castle, which these days looks anything but new, with only a few upright stone wall sections still remaining, was built in the 1200s by the MacDougalls of Lorn (see Dunstaffnage Castle and Castle Stalker). Lismore would have been important to the MacDougall lordship, as already existing on Lismore was Saint Moluag's Cathedral, being the residence of the Bishops of Argyll, and it was important to keep well in with that lot. That lot though had rather a rough start on the island being horribly slaughtered by the Vikings who shortly after their arrival had burned the monks alive in their church, and who didn't really see the point of them (or indeed anyone else) being on their newly acquired Lismore. For awhile it was a cleric free island. There is a tale that centuries earlier in AD 562 Saint Columba (of Iona Abbey fame) and his pal Saint Moluag were both keen to claim Lismore in the name of Christ, racing competitively towards the isle in their little curraghs (best look that one up). Columba was in the lead, (all bets on Columba), so Moluag chopped off one of his fingers and lobbed it ahead of him onto the shore claiming the island before Columba could. Yes, well we all know religion can do funny things to some people.

As history would show the MacDougalls had backed the wrong horse by supporting the puppet King John Balliol, and hence also King Edward I of England, which brought Clan MacDougall head to head with the new King Robert the Bruce at the Battle of Dail Righ in 1306 which they won, and then the Battle of Brander Pass in 1308, which they didn't (see Dunstaffnage Castle and Castle Stalker), resulting in them forfeiting lands, castles, titles and much else.

Coeffin does not enter the history books much at all but it is recorded that it was granted to Sir Colin Campbell of Glenorchy, by another Colin Campbell, the boss, and 1st Earl of Argyll (see Castle Gloom). The Campbells had supported the Bruce during the Wars of Independence, through the loyalty of Sir Neil Campbell of Lochawe, resulting in lands and wealth being granted to the clan by the Hero King.

It is later recorded in 1630 that some Carmichaels of Lismore, had murdered the Bishop of Lismore in 1500s, thus ensuring that no bishop ever set foot on the island again. The Carmichaels of Lismore also used a red & black boat for sheep and cattle stealing activities. Their vessel was painted black on one side for sailing up Loch Linnhe past Coeffin Castle, and painted red on the other side for sailing back, avoiding recognition as the same boat, whilst full of livestock stolen from rival clans. You can still see red and black vessels sailing by carrying livestock but now they are more recognizable with Caledonian MacBrayne painted on the side. They are also a hell of a lot bigger.

As mentioned very little remains of the castle, but there are the scant remains of a bailey wall, and a rectangular great hall measuring 20.5 metres (67 ft) by 10.5 metres (34 ft), so the building was a reasonable size, and with walls 2.5 metres thick (8 ft). Clearly it was a substantial fortress. According to a study and diagrams of Caisteal Chaifein by Alexander Carmichael in 1870, a dungeon had also been excavated but no grizzly stories are forthcoming regarding it's use. He also records that the daughter of a Norwegian king was buried at the caisteal, and further that the caisteal is haunted by the ghost of a maid in a green dress. Adjacent are the overgrown and even more ruinous ruins of the original Viking stone fort.

Aug 2000

DUNTULM CASTLE

Mad MacDonald's final view

On the north western coast of the Isle of Skye with the mountains of the Isle of Harris in the distance over the sea and far away is a cliff top ruin, being the lonely remains of Duntulm Castle. Originally the site of an old Iron Age fort and thereafter used by the Norsemen during their lengthy and violent campaign against the west coast of Scotland, Duntulm was centuries later occupied by the MacLeods of Dunvegan (see Dunvegan Castle) but following disputes over the Skye lands of Trotternish, the castle passed to the MacDonalds of Sleat in the early 17th century. Duntulm is reputed to be haunted by several ghosts, the most notorious being one Hugh MacDonald who in 17th century lived in his own castle, Caisteal Uisdean, some miles south of Duntulm and from where he conducted his piracy activities attacking fishing boats and indeed just about anything else he set his eyes on, bad doings for which he was eventually outlawed. Undeterred, and quite ambitious he desired to be chief of the MacDonalds in place of the 8th Chief, who happened to be his own cousin, Donald Gorm MacDonald, but to achieve such he must dispose of his relatives and so he cunningly invited them to a grand feast in his own castle where they would all be horribly murdered by hired assassins. Now here comes a real historical screw up, of Royal Mail efficiency and delivery proportions. In error, the dinner invitation was sent to the assassins, and the murder instructions were delivered to the MacDonalds at Duntulm. When the Royal Mail's recorded delivery error came to light Hugh wisely got to hell off Skye but was eagerly pursued by the might of Clan MacDonald and he was eventually captured in North Uist, and thereafter was sent back and imprisoned in Duntulm where he was given a jug and plate of beef. The starving villain got stuck in only to discover that the beef was very heavily salted and the jug totally empty. He died alone crazed with thirst and his screams of madness can still be heard from the ruinous remnants of that cliff top dungeon. It is said that the ruin is also haunted by his intended victim, the 8th Chief, Donald Gorm, who being a rather jolly fellow, frequently held wild and debauched parties long into the night. It is quite likely his boisterous laughter drowns out his cousin's screams, particularly on Saturday nights.

The third spectre is 'one eyed' Margaret, who was the sister of the Clan Chief of MacLeod of Dunvegan and who married one of the many MacDonald Lords, either before, during, or after the endless tussles these 2 clans endured. Margaret unfortunately lost an eye in an accident and MacDonald who preferred his wife to have two eyes chucked her out and sent her back to Dunvegan Castle on a one eyed horse, accompanied by a one eyed servant, and a one eyed dog. It is not known what the terms of the guarantee / warranty were and if MacDonald ever received a replacement two eyed female MacLeod.

Similar to Dunskey Castle in Galloway there was definite room for improvement in the interview process of nurse maids, as in a likewise situation here, another baby was accidentally dropped out of a window above the cliffs and ended up a little bit dead on the rocks below. Whilst the Dunskey maid, threw herself out of the window with guilt (albeit fearing this was the safer option), in this case the unfortunate nurse was horribly murdered and locals say her screams can still be heard from the ruins to this day. Recent changes in employment law now prevent this course of action in disciplining careless nursing staff.

Duntulm was built in a highly defendable position on a crag with slopes and cliffs on 3 sides and a dry ditch on the fourth landward side. It was occupied until 1730 when the MacDonalds moved to their newly built Monkstadt House a few miles south, most likely to escape from the numerous ghosts and spirits formally applying for long term residence at the castle. The principle qualification required was of course being dead although the following was advertised locally 'Experience in screaming an advantage. All spectres considered for the position'.

Mar 2008

GREYFRIARS GRAVEYARD

The Evil Judge Mackenzie

Somewhat better known for a loyal wee dog called Bobby, a Skye terrier who for 14 years guarded his master's grave and indeed saw his own canine days out there in 1872 (check out old Disney films albeit this story is a true one just like 101 Dalmations), there is a much darker side to Greyfriars Kirkyard (Graveyard) situated in the old part of Edinburgh.

Sir George Mackenzie a prominent Scottish lawyer was not the sort of man you would want to fall foul of. Having successfully tried and executed many innocent folk in the ridiculous belief that they were witches in the early 1660s, he went on to bigger and better things as Lord Advocate when appointed by Charles II he was put in charge of persecuting the last remaining outlawed Presbyterian Covenanters who opposed Charles' religious views (see Castle Gloom). Following the Battle of Bothwell in 1679, Mackenzie imprisoned some 1,200 Covenanters on rough ground adjacent to Greyfriars Kirkyard where the conditions were incredibly inhumane with most of the prisoners dying from maltreatment, starvation, lack of water and illness whereas it could almost be said that the lucky ones were those executed albeit their severed heads were displayed on spikes around the prison walls being a somewhat poor attempt at landscaping. Such treatment gave the non-forgiving judge the justifiable nickname of Bluidy Mackenzie. His arrogance even extended to himself suggesting there should be a statue of him riding behind Charles II in Parliament Square.

When he died in 1691, he had in somewhat bad taste decided that his final resting place would be in the same place where hundreds had perished on his account, and he has clearly still not left the vicinity and to this day haunts Greyfriars Kirkyard.

In 1999 a poor homeless fellow sought refuge from a wild stormy night in Mackenzie's Black Mausoleum in Greyfriars as the doors were wide open which was most unusual, and from various differing accounts this poor man somehow released the evil spirit of Bluidy. Over a 6 year period between 1999 and 2005 there were 350 documented attacks on visitors and tourists to the graveyard, with no less than 170 collapsing. Many individuals have been bloodied, punched, kicked, pushed, bruised and a few have even had fingers broken all by an unseen aggressor. In addition at times there is a surprising number of dead animals littered around the mausoleum and various poltergeist activity. It all became so concerning with that many witnessed reports of incidents that Edinburgh City Council permanently locked the mausoleum doors and fenced it off but such measures have not kept Bluidy incarcerated in his grim dark home so when visiting Greyfriars DON'T GO ALONE and check the supernatural clause conditions in your medical insurance policy.

Whilst a few legal eagles suggest he did good by donating over 1,000 books and papers on legal stuff, such cannot exactly be looked on as a pardon for his grotesque cruelty. It is to be expected that much of this documentation was hardly pleasant reading anyway and the rest bluidy boring.

AMC 1977

March 2021

Mackenzie's Doorway to Hell

EPILOGUE

Ok, now that you have (probably) read (some of) this book you will be able to address eight great misconceptions in Scottish history in resolving heated debates, these being:

1. Hadrian's Wall was never actually the border between Scotland and England although certain delusional politicians are worryingly planning something similar for the near future.

2. MacBeth was one of Scotland's most honourable kings tragically trashed by one Bill Shakespeare writing a lot of defamatory rubbish about him. Indeed a real 'tragedy'.

3. Robert the Bruce never had a pet spider.

4. Culloden was not a battle between the Scottish and the English but the final disastrous act of a petulant little pillock affectionately known as Bonnie Prince Charlie.

5. There were MacDonalds castles in Scotland centuries before McDonalds diners in downtown Chicago.

6. Stewart is the correct Scottish spelling. Stuart was introduced by Mary Queen of Scots when in France as the French couldn't pronounce Stewart although they soon got their heads around 'Le Weekend'.

7. The Scots were never a unified race and 2,000 years of history (even to the present day) reveals much more of Scot v Scot than ever Scot v English. If in doubt read this book.

8. Scots are a race of people. Scotch is the Water of Life.

So there you have it. 50 interesting places to visit but why stop at 50? The 51st place to visit is the pub nearest to you. Most pubs have a bit of history even if it's only the police raid a couple of weeks ago.

HISTORY AS IT SHOULD BE TOLD

 **ENJOY THIS SCOTLAND**